Animal Biology

STEVE PARKER

PRENTICE HALL

New York   London   Toronto   Sydney   Tokyo   Singapore

ANIMAL BIOLOGY

Managing Editor: Lionel Bender
Art Editor: Ben White
Text Editor: John Stidworthy
Assistant Editor: Madeleine Samuel
Project Editor: Graham Bateman
Production: Clive Sparling

Media conversion and typesetting
Peter MacDonald and Partners and
Brian Blackmore

AN ANDROMEDA BOOK

Devised and produced by:
Andromeda Oxford Ltd
11–15 The Vineyard
Abingdon
Oxfordshire OX14 3PX
England

Prepared by Lionheart Books

Library of Congress Catalog Card
Number: 91-67001

ISBN 0-13-033408-1

Published in North America by:
Prentice Hall General Reference
15 Columbus Circle
New York, New York 10023

PRENTICE HALL and colophon are
registered trademarks of Simon &
Schuster, Inc.

Origination by Alpha Reprographics
Ltd,
Harefield, Middx, England
Manufactured in **Singapore**

10 9 8 7 6 5 4 3 2 1

First Prentice Hall Edition

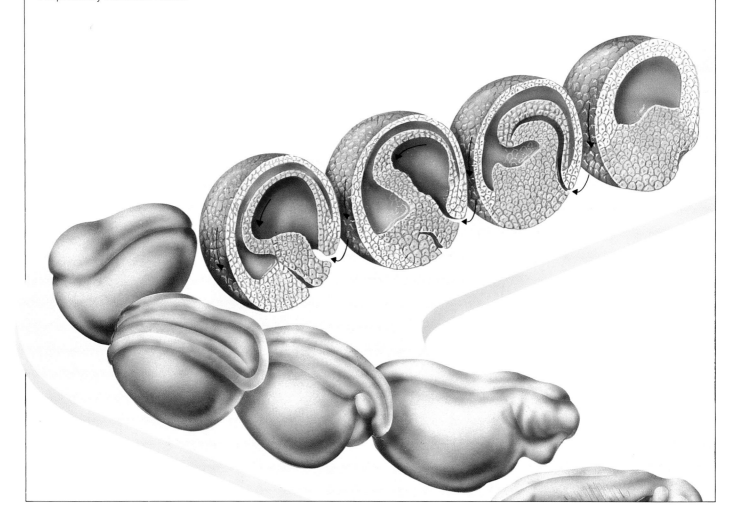

CONTENTS

INTRODUCTION

Biology is the study of living things. It is concerned with plants, animals and micro-organisms and is divided into many subject areas, such as ecology, evolution and behavior. This book is concerned with two major aspects with respect to animals only. The first aspect is anatomy, the detailed structure of the body based on cells, the building blocks of all creatures. The second aspect is physiology, which deals with how animals work – how they feed, move, breathe, coordinate and maintain body control, grow and reproduce.

The book is divided into several sections. The first surveys the animal kingdom and on what basis biologists group different types of animals into families, genera and species or separate kinds. The second section looks at the typical animal cell, how some animals are single-celled and others multi-celled, and it how cells are arranged into tissues and organs. The third, and largest, section deals in turn with the main body functions and organ systems of animals and explains what they do and how they work. The last section deals with growth and reproduction, and includes a discussion of genetics and heredity, plus biotechnology.

Each article in this book is devoted to a specific aspect of the subject. The text starts with a short scene-setting story that highlights one or two of the topics described in the article. It then continues with details of the most interesting aspects, illustrating the discussion with specific examples.

Within the main text and photo captions in each article, the common or everyday names of animals and plants are used. For species illustrated in major artworks but not described elsewhere, the common and scientific (Latin) names of species are given in the caption accompanying the artwork. The index, which provides easy access to text and illustrations, is set out in alphabetical order of common names and of animal and plant groupings with the scientific names of species shown in parentheses.

A glossary provides definitions and short explanations of important technical terms used in the book. There is also a Further Reading list giving details of books for those who wish to take the subject further.

◄A herd of Northern elephant seals (*Mirounga angustirostris*) protected from the Sun's heat by a layer of sand thrown on to their backs.

THE ANIMAL KINGDOM

A child peers into a rock pool. Seaweed fronds grow up towards the surface, and sway back and forth with the movement of water. They feel slippery. Even when touched they still sway. Beside them is a flower-like object. The child goes to touch it. Suddenly, the "flower" shrinks to a blob of jelly. It is an animal, a sea anemone, and can move.

Animals are amazingly varied. They range from microscopic blobs of "jelly" to gigantic whales, from slow-moving slugs to acrobatic eagles, and from flower-like anemones to spiny hedgehogs and thin worms.

Defining an animal is more awkward than it might seem. In general, animals are living things that breathe, move about, feed, and breed to produce more of their kind. But there are many exceptions. Bryozoans (moss animals) do not move about, they are stuck to a rock or piece of seaweed. Mayflies do not feed, at least after they change from larvae to adults, because they have no mouths – they die within a few days.

SORTING INTO GROUPS
In order to talk about animals, it is necessary to have ways of grouping and naming them. Over the past three centuries, scientists have devised the following scheme for making sense of nature's bewildering variety.

The basic group is the species. For example, all tigers are in one species. All lions are put in another species.

▶All animals need plants. Some, including zebra, feed on plants. Other animals, like the lion, feed on plant-eating animals. Animals also find shelter and nesting places among plants. Plants need animals too. Animals enrich the soil with their dung, and aerate it with their burrows. Some help pollinate flowers or spread seeds. All living things depend on each other.

Individual lions vary in size, color and strength, and males have manes whereas females do not. But they all look generally similar, and the male and female lions breed together and produce more lions. Being able to breed together, to produce more of their kind, is the way you can tell that animals are of one species. Animals from different species cannot do this.

Similar species, in turn, are put together in larger groups. These are known as genera (singular: genus).

Lions, tigers, leopards and jaguars are put together in one genus, known as the "big cats."

In turn, genera are put together into larger groups known as families, and families are grouped into orders. The orders are combined into classes, and the classes are grouped into phyla (singular: phylum). About 38 of these main groups, or phyla, make up the Animal Kingdom. Some of these groups live only in the sea. (The main ones are shown on page 9.)

Animal or plant?
These two living things look similar, but one is an animal and one is a plant. Plants like the red *Corallina* seaweed (left) use the Sun's light energy to grow. They trap the light energy by the process of photosynthesis to make their own food, combining simple minerals and nutrients into more complicated substances. Animals, including corals (right), cannot make their own food. They must take in energy-containing nutrients in the form of ready-made food.

NAMING ORGANISMS

Not everyone calls a lion "lion." In the German language it is "löwe." In the Swahili tongue, spoken by people where lions actually live, it is "simba." To avoid confusion, every animal species has its own international scientific name, in two parts.

The first is the name of the genus (generic name) to which that species belongs. For the lion, this is *Panthera*. The second is the name of the species itself (specific name), which is *leo* for the lion. So the lion's full scientific name is *Panthera leo*, and this is the same in all languages. Other big cats in the genus include the tiger, whose name is *Panthera tigris*, and the jaguar, which is *Panthera onca*.

HOW MANY ANIMAL SPECIES?

We do not know how many kinds of animals there are. So far almost 1.5 million animal species have been described and named. New ones are discovered regularly. And there are almost certainly many more waiting to be discovered, in remote places such as tropical forests and mountainsides.

The largest animal group is the insects, with about one million species named so far. Some biologists estimate that there could be 10 times this many insect species which have not yet been discovered. There are about 9,000 species of birds, 4,000 species of mammals, and 37,000 species of molluscs (the phylum that

7

includes snails, slugs, whelks, oysters and octopuses).

Some phyla are very small. There are only about 260 species of lampshells, or brachiopods, which are sea-dwellers resembling clams. There are only a dozen or so species of horseshoe worms, or phoronidans, which also live in the sea. They stay buried in a tube in the mud, and have fan-like tentacles.

ANIMALS AND EVOLUTION
The great majority of biologists believe that animal species, and the species of other living things such as plants and fungi, have not been created separately. They have arisen by evolution – the gradual change of living things over time. The most direct evidence comes from fossils. These are the remains of long-dead animals and plants, preserved in the rocks. Usually only the hard parts are preserved, such as shells and bones.

Life first appeared in its simplest form about 3,000 million years ago. The oldest recognizable fossils of animals are in rocks about 650 million years old. The fossils are very rare and faint. Even so, these ancient animals were already quite complicated, and so they had probably been evolving for a long time before that.

The most complete fossil record is of the vertebrates – the animals with backbones. Fossils show the fish appearing first, then amphibians, then reptiles, and finally the birds and mammals. There are various animals that show links between these groups. For example, the earliest known amphibians were very much like a group of fishes that had appeared not long before. These links strongly suggest a process of evolution.

ANIMALS AROUND THE WORLD
Animals live in almost every place on Earth, from the snowy wastes of the poles, to steaming hot tropical forests, to high mountains, to the deepest oceans. Evolution has shaped the features of an animal so that it is suited to certain conditions. We would not expect to find penguins in a desert, or a pond worm in a tree-top. Each species survives best in a certain place, known as its habitat.

Just as they differ on the outside in looks, color and shape, so animals differ on the inside. However, their bodies have to carry out the same basic life processes, such as feeding, breathing, moving and breeding. The following sections of this book look at each of these main processes in turn, and show how various animal groups have solved the many varied problems of living.

◄Some animals manage to survive in extreme conditions. These Australian soldier crabs can cope with the hot Sun, salty sea water, fresh rainwater and drying winds. They are really well suited to their surroundings.

►We make sense of the natural world by grouping together living things that show similarities. There are several grouping systems. The one shown here has five main groups or kingdoms. The Animal Kingdom is the largest.

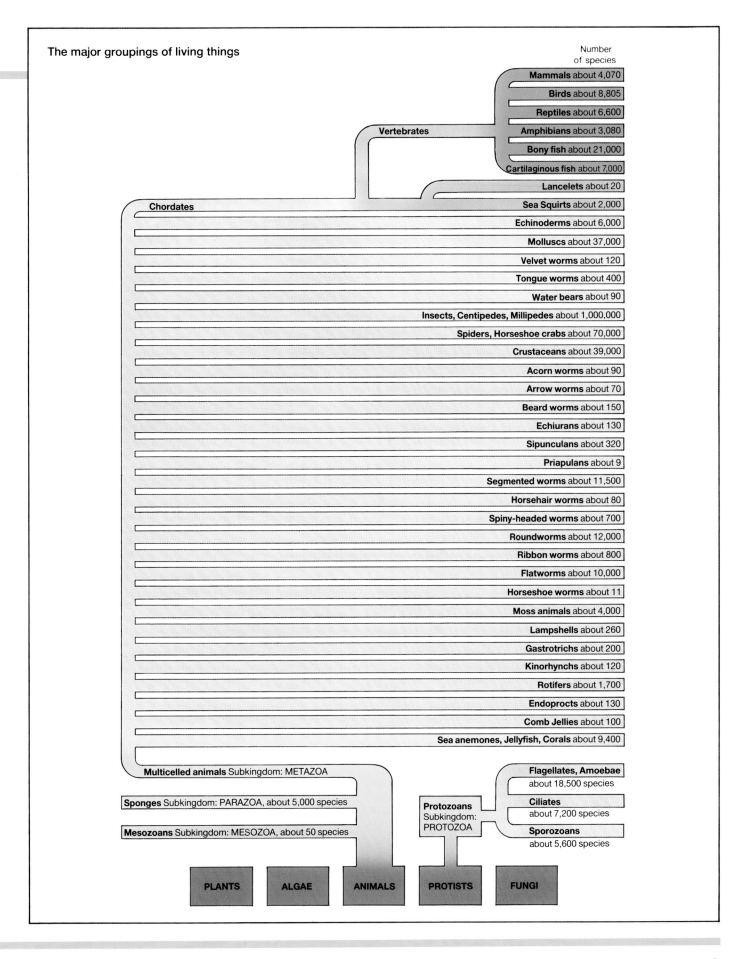

Number of species

Mammals about 4,070
Birds about 8,805
Reptiles about 6,600
Amphibians about 3,080
Bony fish about 21,000
Cartilaginous fish about 7,000

Vertebrates

Lancelets about 20
Sea Squirts about 2,000

Chordates

Echinoderms about 6,000
Molluscs about 37,000
Velvet worms about 120
Tongue worms about 400
Water bears about 90
Insects, Centipedes, Millipedes about 1,000,000
Spiders, Horseshoe crabs about 70,000
Crustaceans about 39,000
Acorn worms about 90
Arrow worms about 70
Beard worms about 150
Echiurans about 130
Sipunculans about 320
Priapulans about 9
Segmented worms about 11,500
Horsehair worms about 80
Spiny-headed worms about 700
Roundworms about 12,000
Ribbon worms about 800
Flatworms about 10,000
Horseshoe worms about 11
Moss animals about 4,000
Lampshells about 260
Gastrotrichs about 200
Kinorhynchs about 120
Rotifers about 1,700
Endoprocts about 130
Comb Jellies about 100
Sea anemones, Jellyfish, Corals about 9,400

Multicelled animals Subkingdom: METAZOA

Sponges Subkingdom: PARAZOA, about 5,000 species

Mesozoans Subkingdom: MESOZOA, about 50 species

Protozoans
Subkingdom:
PROTOZOA

Flagellates, Amoebae
about 18,500 species

Ciliates
about 7,200 species

Sporozoans
about 5,600 species

PLANTS   ALGAE   ANIMALS   PROTISTS   FUNGI

CELLS, TISSUES, ORGANS

A scientist looks down her microscope. She is studying how a sea urchin egg develops. As time goes on the single egg divides. Now it consists of two blobs joined together. Soon it is four, then eight, as it keeps dividing. Soon it is difficult to count how many blobs, or cells, it has divided into. The whole adult animal is made up of millions of these cells.

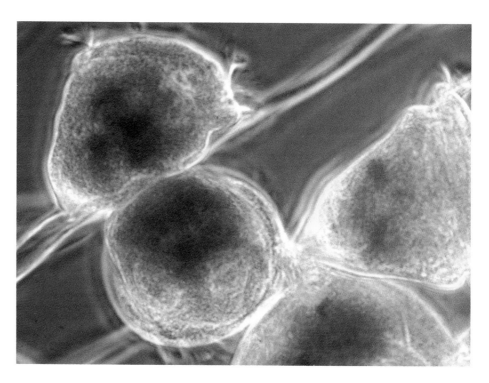

Cells are the basic building blocks of animals. (They also make up plants, fungi and other living things.) The simplest of animals, protozoans, each consist of only one cell.

Larger animals are built from many millions of cells. A human being, for example, consists of around 10 million million cells. These cells are not all the same. There are many different kinds that do different jobs. Nerve cells carry nerve signals. Muscle cells are long and thin, but they can shorten to help an animal move. Red blood cells carry oxygen in the blood. There are about 200 main kinds of cells in an animal such as a human.

THE SIZES OF CELLS
Apart from a few exceptions, cells are very small. The largest single-celled animals, protozoans, are $\frac{1}{10}$in long, and the smallest are about $\frac{1}{2,500}$in (decimal 1μm: one-thousandth of a millimeter) across. Microscopes are needed to study them in detail.

A typical cell in any multi-celled animal is 10 to 20μm across. Bigger animals have more cells than smaller ones. It is as though nature uses bricks of the same size, whether building a small house or a giant skyscraper.

A few highly specialized single cells are much larger, such as birds' eggs. Others are much smaller, for example the doughnut-shaped red blood cell which is only 7μm across and 2μm deep at its thickest.

INSIDE A CELL
The typical animal cell is surrounded by a thin, flexible "skin" called the cell membrane. Inside, a system of microtubules and microfilaments forms the cytoskeleton – the cell's internal "scaffolding." The cytoskeleton gives the cell its basic shape and helps it to change shape as it moves. It controls and channels the movements of all chemicals and substances inside the body of the cell.

There are also several recognizable structures inside a typical cell. These are known as organelles. Each of these does a specific job, as shown opposite. The nucleus contains the genetic instructions for building and maintaining the cell – and indeed, for building and running the whole animal (see page 76). A few very specialized cells, such as red blood cells, do not have a nucleus.

BREAKDOWN AND BUILD-UP
Cells need energy to live. Animals obtain their energy from the food they eat. This is either from plants or other animals. Chemicals in the food are

▲Animals like this amoeba carry out all life's functions in a single cell. They usually live in water, since they have no thick, protective cell wall like a plant cell, and so would soon dry out in air.

▼Animals such as these gemsbok, in Namibia, are made from billions of cells. Tiny contractions of the millions of muscle cells propel the whole animal at speeds of more than 30mph.

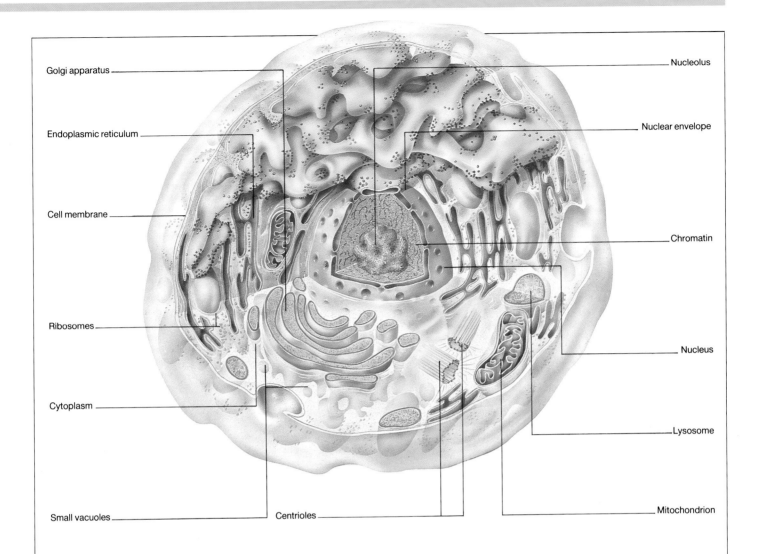

Golgi apparatus

Endoplasmic reticulum

Cell membrane

Ribosomes

Cytoplasm

Small vacuoles

Centrioles

Nucleolus

Nuclear envelope

Chromatin

Nucleus

Lysosome

Mitochondrion

Structure of a cell

This general diagram of an animal cell shows that it is not a mass of jelly, but has a complicated internal structure. Various organelles can be seen within. The main one is the nucleus, the control center of the cell, which also houses the genetic information. It is surrounded by its nuclear envelope. Another, larger membrane surrounds the whole cell and forms its "skin." These membranes are not total barriers, but partial ones. They allow certain substances to pass through, such as nutrients on their way in, and wastes on their way out. The thin, clear fluid between the organelles is known as cytoplasm.

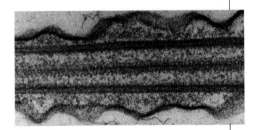

4

1

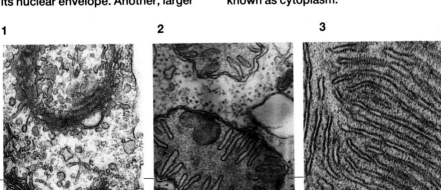

2

3

◀▲Organelles under the powerful electron microscope. Golgi bodies (1) make secretions such as mucus and digestive juices. Mitochondria (2), the cell's "powerhouses," generate chemical energy from nutrients. Endoplasmic reticulum (3) makes proteins. Microtubules (4) form the cell's skeleton.

Cells and tissues

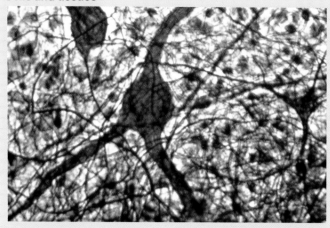

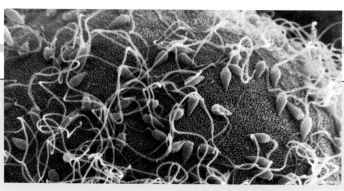

▲Sperm cells are the reproductive cells from the male organs. They are shaped like tadpoles, and the tail lashes to make the sperm swim towards the female egg. The photograph (top) shows swarms of sperm cells from a sea urchin surrounding an egg.

▲▼Nerve cells, or neurons, are long and thin, with many fine branches. They carry the tiny electrical signals that form nerve messages. The myelin sheath speeds the signals on their way along the main "wire," the axon. The photograph shows a network of mouse neurons.

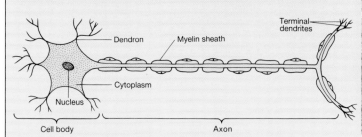

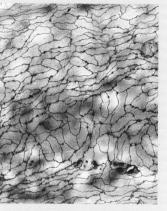

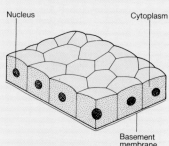

◀▲Epithelial cells cover many body parts, on both the outside and inside. They fit together like crazy-paving (left) or a brick wall (above).

▼There are various forms of connective tissue, such as bone and cartilage. The photograph (below left) shows the circular pattern of human bone under the microscope. The diagram shows areolar tissue, a connective tissue made of cells and elastic fibers.

▼Blood is a type of tissue, although it is in the form of a liquid. It contains several different kinds of blood cells. The red cells carry oxygen.

The various types of white cells help to fight disease. The photograph (bottom) shows two white cells surrounded by red cells.

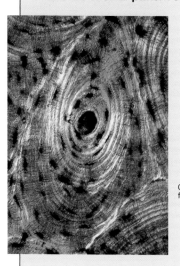

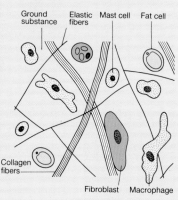

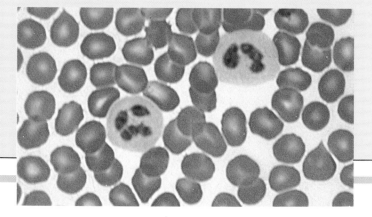

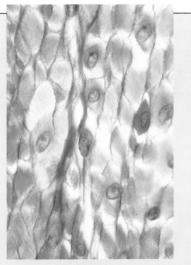

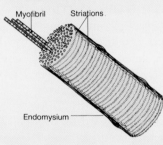

Myofibril · Striations · Endomysium

▲ Muscle cells are bundled together in their thousands to make muscle fibers. The photograph (top) is of muscle cells from a cat's intestine.

broken down to release their energy. They also provide raw materials for building new cells and replacing old or worn-out parts. These changes occur as hundreds of chemical reactions that take place inside cells. These reactions are collectively known as the metabolism.

LIFE AND DEATH

Few cells live for long. A worm's intestinal cell lasts for a few days. A red blood cell has a life of about 3 months. A human bone cell might live for 25 years. In most animals, certain cells are specialized to multiply and form new cells, which replace the old, worn-out or damaged ones. A human skin cell lives for only about a month. It is formed in the multiplying group of cells at the base of the outer skin layer. It gradually passes outwards, becomes hardened and dies. It reaches the skin's surface, and is worn away. The rate of cell multiplication matches the rate of cell loss, so new cells are "born" at the right rate to replace those that "die."

A few cells, such as certain nerve cells, cannot multiply once the animal is fully developed, although they may be repaired if they are damaged.

JOINING FORCES

Similar cells are grouped together into tissues. For example, many long, thin muscle cells lie side by side to form muscle tissue. Many nerve cells, with their networks of branching "wires," are linked together into nerve tissue.

A tissue is specialized to carry out one or more functions. Epithelial tissue acts as a covering for many body parts, both inside and outside the animal. In a complex creature, such as a giraffe, it lines the inside of the mouth and throat, the airways down the windpipe and lungs, and the inside of the stomach, intestines and other digestive parts. It is usually made of cells that multiply at a fast rate, so replacing those cells which are rubbed off or die on the surface.

SUPER-CELLS

Muscle tissue is specialized to contract, or get shorter. The giant molecules inside it move past each other like ratchets, making the cells shorter. In fact muscle is slightly more complicated because its "cells" are actually "super-cells," formed from many individual cells joined together into one larger unit, with many nuclei.

PACKING TISSUES

A relatively simple type of multi-celled animal, such as a jellyfish, consists of only a few types of tissue. A more complicated animal has dozens of tissue types, including several kinds of connective tissues. These are the body's "packaging materials." They surround, support, separate and protect other parts. Their cells are not usually packed tightly together but

◀ The ostrich's egg, before it starts to develop into a chick, is the largest example of a single cell. It weighs over 3lb and is 8in long. Most of this is food stored as yolk, to feed the growing baby bird.

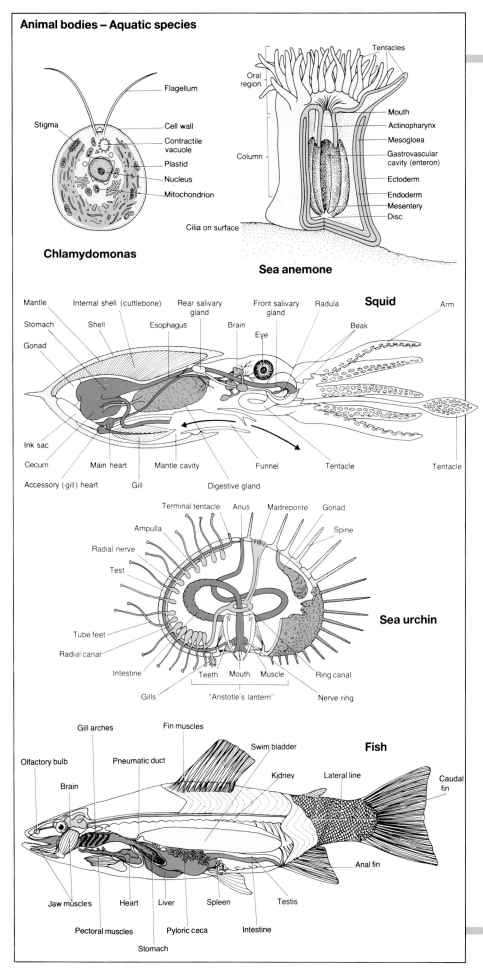

Animal bodies – Aquatic species

Chlamydomonas

- Flagellum
- Stigma
- Cell wall
- Contractile vacuole
- Plastid
- Nucleus
- Mitochondrion
- Cilia on surface

Sea anemone

- Tentacles
- Oral region
- Mouth
- Actinopharynx
- Mesogloea
- Column
- Gastrovascular cavity (enteron)
- Ectoderm
- Endoderm
- Mesentery
- Disc

Squid

- Mantle
- Internal shell (cuttlebone)
- Rear salivary gland
- Front salivary gland
- Radula
- Arm
- Stomach
- Shell
- Esophagus
- Brain
- Beak
- Gonad
- Eye
- Ink sac
- Cecum
- Main heart
- Mantle cavity
- Funnel
- Tentacle
- Tentacle
- Accessory (gill) heart
- Gill
- Digestive gland

Sea urchin

- Terminal tentacle
- Anus
- Madreporite
- Gonad
- Ampulla
- Spine
- Radial nerve
- Test
- Tube feet
- Radial canal
- Intestine
- Teeth
- Mouth
- Muscle
- Ring canal
- Gills
- "Aristotle's lantern"
- Nerve ring

Fish

- Gill arches
- Fin muscles
- Swim bladder
- Olfactory bulb
- Pneumatic duct
- Kidney
- Lateral line
- Brain
- Caudal fin
- Anal fin
- Jaw muscles
- Heart
- Liver
- Spleen
- Testis
- Pectoral muscles
- Pyloric ceca
- Intestine
- Stomach

scattered about, embedded in a "background" substance known as the ground-tissue or matrix.

The different kinds of connective tissue have different types of cells and matrices. In areolar connective tissue there is a tangle of slender fibers with various cells dotted about. In adipose connective tissue some of the cells are swollen with blobs of fat. In fibrous connective tissue the fibers are much more numerous and arranged as bundles or sheets. Two other types of connective tissue are the bone and cartilage of the skeleton.

GETTING ORGANIZED

An organ is one main "part" of an animal, such as the brain, heart, stomach or kidney. Each organ is usually made up of several types of tissue that work together to do one important job in the animal's body. A simple animal like a sponge has no parts that could be called organs. A complicated animal such as a fish or bird has many organs.

The brain is the organ that controls and coordinates the whole body. The heart is a muscular organ that pumps blood. The stomach is a digestive organ that pulps food and dissolves it with powerful chemicals. The kidneys are filtering organs that remove waste substances from blood.

The same tissues can occur in different organs. For instance, the brain is chiefly nerve tissue, but also contains blood vessels and connective tissue. A muscle is mainly muscle tissue but it is also has blood vessels and controlling nerves, as well as connective tissue.

ALL SYSTEMS GO

The more complicated animals have organs that are linked together into

◀These diagrams show the main internal parts of different water animals. Chlamydomonas (top left) is a single cell. All the others are multi-celled and some have many different organs.

systems. A system is a group of organs that works together, to carry out one of the main functions of a "living thing" – for example its breathing, feeding, breeding, or excretion.

The circulatory system of a human is one example. It consists of the heart as the pump, the large blood vessels known as arteries and veins, the smaller blood vessels called capillaries, and the blood which flows continuously around the system.

Another example is the digestive system. Its organs vary from one kind of animal to another. In mammals such as ourselves it consists of a mouth for taking in food, a stomach for mashing it up and digesting it, a small intestine for the job of absorbing nutrients, and a large intestine for dealing with the left-over wastes.

Not all organs of a system are found near to each other in the body, or even joined to each other in an obvious way, as in the digestive system. In fact the circulatory system, and others such as the hormonal system and the nervous system, are spread throughout the body.

WHOLE ANIMALS

The following sections of this book look at the way in which the vast variety of animals carry out the essentials of life. In small and simple creatures such as amoebas, everything goes on within a single cell. In large and complex creatures such as fish, frogs and mammals, there are hundreds of tissues, organized into many organs, which are grouped into a few main systems. There are many ways in which an animal's body can be organized. Each phylum is different. But the end result is the same: a fully functioning animal.

▶The main internal organs of land-dwellers. Each has a heart to pump blood, lungs for breathing, and a skeleton made of bones. The digestive organs differ: a bird has a large crop to store food.

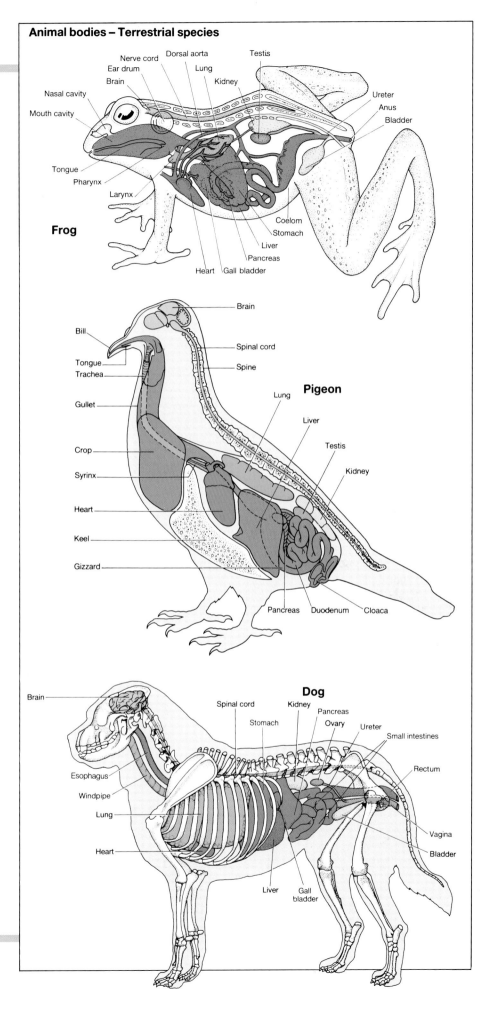

RESPIRATION

Hunting in the ocean depths, a hungry young Sperm whale comes upon its deadly enemy, a Giant squid. The two animals grapple, and the squid squirms as the whale tries in vain to seize it in sharp-toothed jaws. Soon the whale realizes its mistake, but the squid now holds it with powerful suckered arms. The whale begins to gasp – it needs air. But the squid hangs on, and the whale drowns.

Humans and many other animals take breathing for granted. We do not have to think about it. The movements of breathing happen automatically, even when we sleep. But what is breathing for, and how does it take place?

BODY CHEMISTRY
The chemical reactions inside an animal's body rely on a constant supply of energy. This energy is contained in food (page 22). But once inside the body, the food must be changed into a suitable form to power the various chemical reactions.

The usual way of doing this is to combine the energy-containing food with oxygen, in a series of chemical stages known as metabolic respiration. During the sequence, energy is transferred onwards to other chemical reactions and used. At the end there are leftover waste products such as carbon dioxide and water, which contain little or no energy.

Chemical reactions are happening all the time in a living thing. So a constant supply of oxygen is required. Oxygen as a gas makes up one-fifth of the air, and it is also dissolved in water. Extracting oxygen from air or water is therefore a vital part of staying alive.

SMALL AND SIMPLE
Oxygen does not stay still. It is always spreading around, "seeping" from

places where it is concentrated to places where its levels are lower. This process is called diffusion.

The inside of a small and simple organism such as an amoeba has low oxygen levels, since it is always using up oxygen in respiration. Therefore new supplies of oxygen tend to pass into the amoeba's body from the water around it, through its very thin "skin." Diffusion is a slow process, but the amoeba's oxygen needs are very small, and its body is also very small. Diffusion is fast enough to keep pace.

As the oxygen near to the amoeba is used up, so more oxygen diffuses towards it from the surrounding water. The waste products from the amoeba, such as carbon dioxide, travel in the opposite direction. As their levels build up inside its body, they diffuse out through its skin.

PROBLEMS OF BEING BIG
The inside of a larger animal is also continually using up oxygen. But size brings several problems. One is that a bigger creature usually has a thick, protective covering, such as a fish's scales or a mammal's furry skin. Oxygen cannot pass easily through these coverings.

Another problem is that parts of a big animal are some distance from its outside. Oxygen would take too long to diffuse over such a distance. Also, larger animals use up more oxygen than tiny ones. As they do so, the air or water around them becomes oxygen-poor and "stale." Diffusion cannot work fast enough to bring in more oxygen from the surroundings and make the air or water oxygen-rich and "fresh" again.

BIGGER MEANS LESS
A small organism like an amoeba has a relatively large surface area ("skin" area) compared to the volume of its body. So there is plenty of surface through which oxygen can enter. Bigger animals have less surface area

▲ **Some air-breathing animals in water** Some animals breathe air, yet spend much or all of their time under water: King penguin (*Aptenodytes patagonicus*) **(1)**, the larva of a mosquito (*Culex* species) **(2)** and a damselfly (*Coenagrion* species) **(3)**, Yellow-bellied sea snake (*Pelamis platurus*) **(4)**, and Blue whale (*Balaenoptera musculus*) **(5)**.

▶ The European grayling. Just behind its eyes lie the bony opercula, the gill covers. Water enters the mouth, passes over the gills – where gas exchange takes place – then leaves via the gill slits.

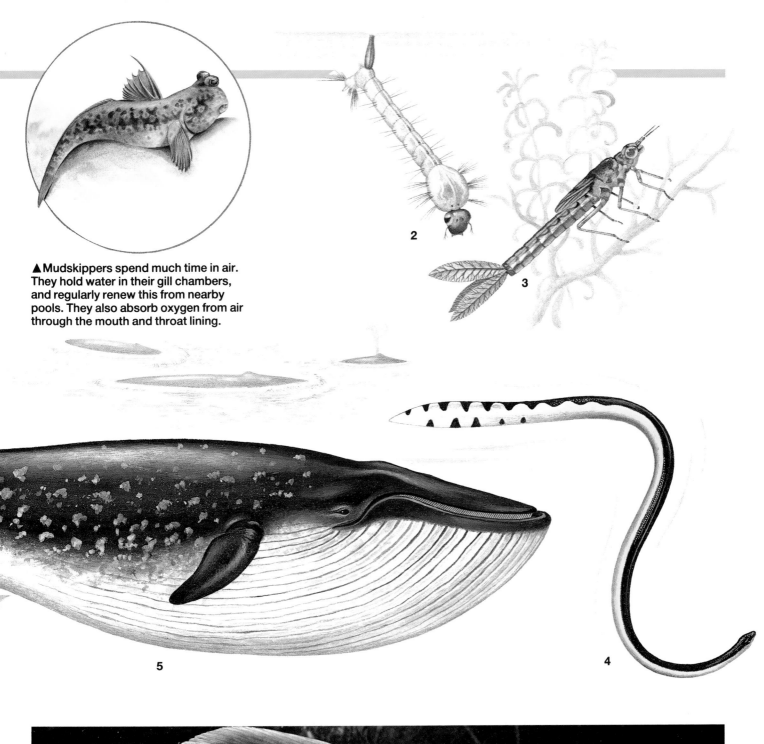

▲ Mudskippers spend much time in air. They hold water in their gill chambers, and regularly renew this from nearby pools. They also absorb oxygen from air through the mouth and throat lining.

2

3

4

5

compared to their volume. Although their oxygen needs increase with size, the ability to absorb oxygen through that surface falls in proportion to their bulk.

GILLS AND LUNGS

For these reasons, larger animals have developed many different ways of getting the oxygen they need. Two examples are gills, which absorb oxygen dissolved in water, and lungs, which take in oxygen from the air. Inside the body, the oxygen is distributed by a circulatory system such as the blood network (see page 26). In order to replace stale, oxygen-poor

◄A Water spider in its "diving bell". It brings small air bubbles from the water surface trapped in its body hairs to add to its underwater store of air.

air with a fresh supply, mammals such as ourselves, and birds and reptiles carry out the movements we call "breathing." Old air is blown out of the lungs, and new air is sucked in.

In bigger animals, as in the amoeba, waste carbon dioxide travels in the opposite direction, from the body out into the surroundings. Getting rid of carbon dioxide is just as important as obtaining oxygen, since if the carbon dioxide level builds up in the body, it acts as a poison. This is why the entire process is known as respiratory gas exchange – in effect, swapping carbon dioxide for oxygen.

FROM FLATWORMS TO FISH

Many small water-living animals are like the amoeba. They can absorb sufficient oxygen from the water,

without the need for specialized body parts. Calculations show that most animals up to about $\frac{1}{20}$in in diameter can take in sufficient oxygen by diffusion alone. If larger, they need specialized parts for gas exchange.

Even so, some animals larger than $\frac{1}{20}$in still rely on simple diffusion. They usually have a body which is a series of thin, folded sheets or narrow fingers, as in sea anemones, or they have a very flat, leaf-like shape, as in flatworms. Then no part of the body is more than about $\frac{1}{20}$in from the surrounding water.

Most bigger water-dwellers have gills of some kind. These are outward expansions of the body surface with blood vessels just underneath. They vary in shape from simple cylinders or flaps, as in worms and starfish, to the

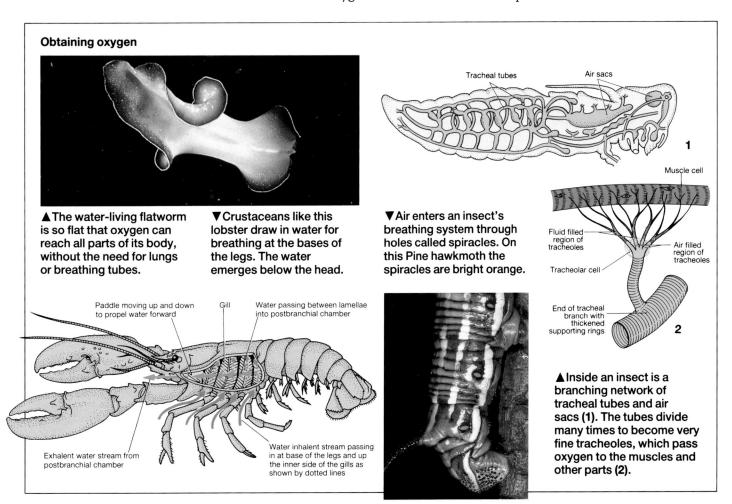

Obtaining oxygen

▲The water-living flatworm is so flat that oxygen can reach all parts of its body, without the need for lungs or breathing tubes.

▼Crustaceans like this lobster draw in water for breathing at the bases of the legs. The water emerges below the head.

▼Air enters an insect's breathing system through holes called spiracles. On this Pine hawkmoth the spiracles are bright orange.

Tracheal tubes   Air sacs

1

Muscle cell

Fluid filled region of tracheoles

Air filled region of tracheoles

Tracheolar cell

End of tracheal branch with thickened supporting rings

2

▲Inside an insect is a branching network of tracheal tubes and air sacs (1). The tubes divide many times to become very fine tracheoles, which pass oxygen to the muscles and other parts (2).

Paddle moving up and down to propel water forward

Gill

Water passing between lamellae into postbranchial chamber

Exhalent water stream from postbranchial chamber

Water inhalent stream passing in at base of the legs and up the inner side of the gills as shown by dotted lines

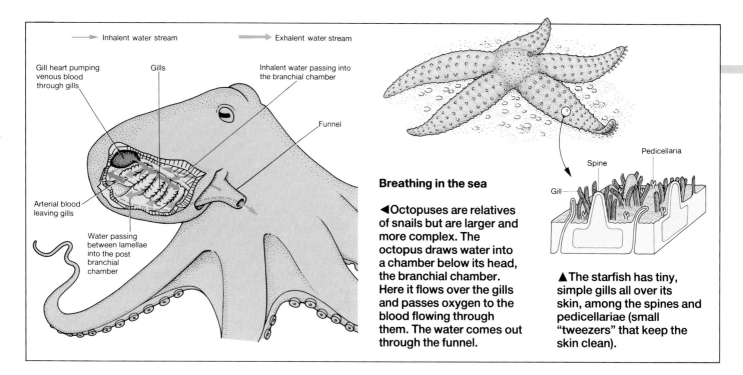

Inhalent water stream → Exhalent water stream →

Gill heart pumping venous blood through gills

Gills

Inhalent water passing into the branchial chamber

Funnel

Arterial blood leaving gills

Water passing between lamellae into the post branchial chamber

Breathing in the sea

◄Octopuses are relatives of snails but are larger and more complex. The octopus draws water into a chamber below its head, the branchial chamber. Here it flows over the gills and passes oxygen to the blood flowing through them. The water comes out through the funnel.

Spine

Pedicellaria

Gill

▲The starfish has tiny, simple gills all over its skin, among the spines and pedicellariae (small "tweezers" that keep the skin clean).

complicated feathery gills found in crabs, fish and some molluscs.

BREATHING UNDER WATER

Delicate, feathery gills, packed with fine blood vessels, are likely to get damaged unless they are well protected. In little animals such as the young tadpole, this is not too hazardous. The gills are fluffy-looking tufts on either side of the head, but they are very small, and they soon shrink away as the tadpole's lungs develop for breathing air.

Bigger creatures have more of a problem. In the octopus, the gills are safe inside the main space in the body, known as the mantle cavity. In most fish, they are under a hard, bony flap known as the operculum on the side of the "neck." In a crab, they are along the sides of the body, under the hard outer shell.

However, enclosing and protecting the gills means that water can no longer flow freely past them. So these types of animals have pumping systems that force a flow of fresh, oxygen-rich water past their gills. Water is a dense, "syrupy" substance compared to air. It would be difficult for a water-dweller to take in and then squirt out water, in the way that land animals breathe air in and out. Usually

the water flows in through one opening, passes over the gills, and leaves the body through a separate opening.

The pumping equipment varies between the main groups of animals. In molluscs like the octopus, it is the pulsating muscular walls of the chamber housing the gills. Crustaceans such as the lobster have beating, paddle-like structures. Fish use rhythmic expansion and contraction of the mouth and gill chambers. Swimming forwards also causes water to pass over the fish's gills.

LIVING ON LAND

Most bigger land-dwellers have lungs of some kind. These are infoldings of the body surface with blood vessels just under their lining. In their simple form, as in land snails, they are hollow chambers with walls that are not folded. In more complex versions the lung has folds or tunnels or finely branched tubes, to increase the surface area for absorbing oxygen.

Insects do not have proper lungs. They are small enough to rely on a form of diffusion. Oxygen diffuses into the air in a network of tiny tubes within their bodies. The tubes branch and reach every body part. However, this system is one of the reasons why most insects are small. The oxygen

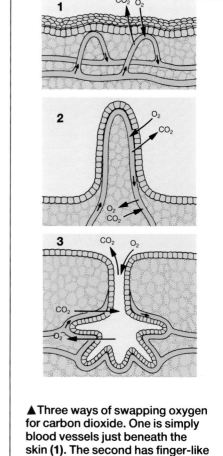

▲Three ways of swapping oxygen for carbon dioxide. One is simply blood vessels just beneath the skin (1). The second has finger-like projections from the surface with blood vessels inside (2), as in fish gills. The third is a hole leading to a chamber with blood vessels just under its lining (3), forming a lung.

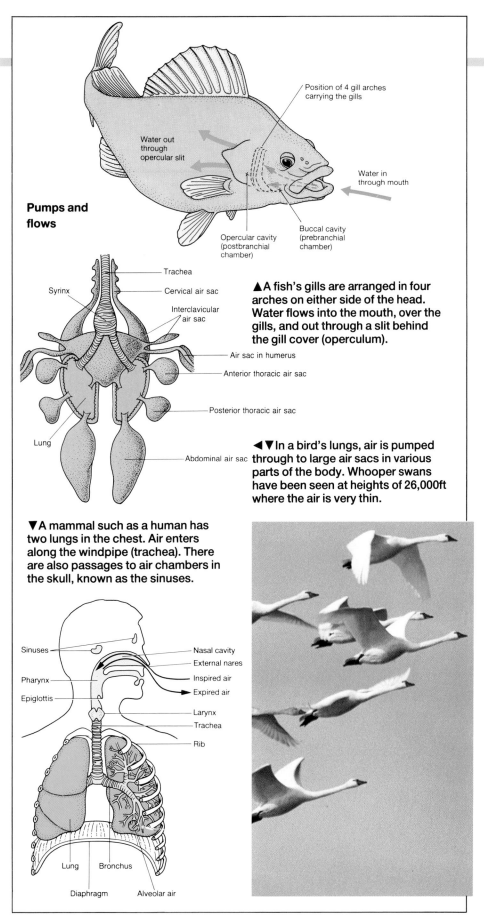

Pumps and flows

▲A fish's gills are arranged in four arches on either side of the head. Water flows into the mouth, over the gills, and out through a slit behind the gill cover (operculum).

◄▼In a bird's lungs, air is pumped through to large air sacs in various parts of the body. Whooper swans have been seen at heights of 26,000ft where the air is very thin.

▼A mammal such as a human has two lungs in the chest. Air enters along the windpipe (trachea). There are also passages to air chambers in the skull, known as the sinuses.

can diffuse only a matter of a few tenths of an inch. The biggest insects, such as the Goliath beetle, are at the size limit for its efficiency. However, the insect's body movements help to squeeze stale air out and suck fresh air back into the tubes.

THE BREATH OF LIFE

All the vertebrate land animals (those with backbones) have a pumping system to move air in and out of the lungs. Amphibians use the floor of the mouth and throat as a pump. Its up and down movement is a familiar sight in many frogs. The nostrils and the throat open and close in time with the pump, to force air into the lungs or allow it to escape.

Reptiles such as lizards, and all mammals – including ourselves – use the chest as a pump. The chest is moved by muscles attached to the ribs and backbone. Mammals also have a diaphragm, a dome-shaped muscle in the floor of the chest. It pulls down the bases of the lungs to increase their volume when breathing in. Inside the spongy lung tissue there are millions of minute air spaces called alveoli, which increase the surface area of the lung many times. Spread out flat, the inner surface of a human lung would cover an area the size of a tennis court.

BREATHING WHEN AIRBORNE

Bird lungs are different from those of other air-breathing vertebrates. They are solid and through them run many parallel tubes called parabronchi. Holes in the walls of these tubes open into very fine air tubes that are surrounded by equally fine blood vessels, giving a great area for absorbing oxygen. Air is moved through the lungs by altering the volume of several thin-walled air sacs in other parts of the bird's body. This system is so efficient at obtaining oxygen that flocks of curlews have been seen in the rarefied air at 33,000ft, higher than the summit of Mount Everest.

FEEDING, DIGESTION

A chameleon sits perfectly still on a branch in an African forest. A fly buzzes past and lands about 8in away. The lizard's eyes slowly swivel, and – snap, the fly is gone. A wildlife film-maker captures the moment on high-speed film. Only when the film is slowed down on playback, can she see the chameleon's long tongue flick out, grab the fly on its sticky tip, and whisk it into the mouth.

Any machine needs fuel to drive it. The animal body is a kind of machine, and its fuel is food. Food provides the energy for powering the chemical reactions of life, and the nutrients for body development, growth, maintenance and repair.

Plants make their own food. They use the energy in sunlight to build complex body tissues from carbon dioxide, water and other simple substances. Animals do the opposite. They take their food into the body. We call this feeding. Then they break the food down into smaller and simpler substances. This process is known as digestion. Finally the substances are absorbed into the body, converted and used for energy or to build new body tissue.

Animals therefore rely on plants for food, directly or indirectly. Some animals, the herbivores, eat plants directly. Others, the carnivores, eat animals. Still others are scavengers, feeding on the dying and dead remains of living things.

SIEVING AND SUCKING

Not all food comes in convenient bite-sized lumps. In the waters of most lakes and seas the main food source is the phytoplankton. This consists of microscopic plants, many of them single-celled. This food is best obtained by filtering or sieving the water. Many water-dwelling animals are filter-feeders. They include such

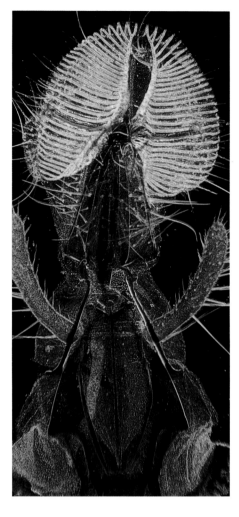

▼The "fan" of the fanworm is used for feeding. Each feathery tentacle filters small bits of food floating in the water and passes them down to the worm's body, which is in a tube part-buried in the mud. If danger threatens, the fan is pulled into the tube.

▲Digestion does not always take place inside the body. This magnified photograph shows a housefly's sponge-like mouthparts. The fly pours digestive juices on to its food. These turn it into a "soup." The fly then mops up the soup and sucks it into the body.

▲▼The Giant amoeba, seen here under the microscope, has a simple feeding method. It simply flows jelly-like arms around the food, in this case a small group of green algae (simple plants), and takes it into its body. This process, known as phagocytosis, is shown step by step in the diagram below.

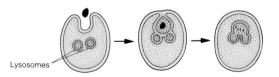

Lysosomes

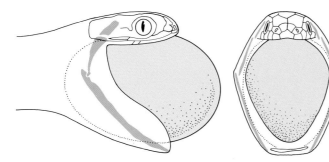

▲▶The African egg-eating snake can swallow an egg more than four times as wide as its head. The bones in its jaws hinge and slide apart to allow the snake to open its mouth so wide. The egg is broken by bones in its throat, and the snake spits out the eggshell.

shellfish as mussels, worms such as fanworms, and also the tiny water fleas and similar creatures that occur in their millions and form the animal part of the plankton.

Animal blood and body fluids, and plant sap and nectar, are food for creatures that suck or pump fluids into their digestive system. Leeches suck the blood of larger animals. Mosquitoes, aphids and similar insects have piercing mouthparts like hollow needles. A butterfly's mouth is a hollow straw for sucking up nectar.

TOUGH TO EAT – OR TO CATCH

On land, many plants grow to a large size, and so herbivores have little trouble in finding them. But plant food such as bark or old leaves is tough, stringy, and hard to eat. Many herbivores have chewing mouthparts or wide, flat teeth, and they spend much time grinding and crushing their food before they swallow it. Because their food is so tough it wears down the teeth. Some herbivorous mammals have teeth that grow continuously from the roots, for example rats and mice. Others, elephants for instance, have teeth that are replaced in sequence throughout the animal's lifetime as they wear out.

Carnivores have to catch their food. They usually have powerful senses to detect prey, and also sharp teeth and claws to seize it, kill it and tear it into

pieces that can be swallowed. However, there are many variations. The Giant anteater has no teeth. It licks up termites and ants with its sticky 24in-long tongue, and grinds this meal with horny plates in the roof of its mouth and in its muscular stomach.

FEEDING TIMES

Plants tend to be less nutritious than meat, and are more difficult to digest. On average, herbivores have to spend more time feeding than carnivores, and they eat more. A snail spends most of each night rasping at plant leaves with its file-like tongue, the radula. In contrast, a snake that captures a large meal may not feed again for many weeks.

WHAT IS IN FOOD?

In many animals, the mouthparts or teeth help to chew and mash lumpy food into a pulp. This is the physical part of digestion. But chemically, the bulk of most foods is made up of giant molecules that animals cannot use directly. These giant molecules are split into smaller ones during digestion. This job is done by digestive enzymes. These enzymes are powerful juices that break the chemical bonds within the molecules and allow them to fall apart.

▲ The elephant is a "fermentation tank on legs." Its leafy food consists of plant cells with thick, tough walls of cellulose (shown inset). Mammals cannot make digestive enzymes that break down cellulose. But the elephant's stomach contains microscopic bacteria which have enzymes that digest cellulose.

▶ The parts of a ruminant mammal's digestive system. Ruminants include cattle, sheep, goats, antelopes, deer and giraffes. The stomach has four main chambers. Food is swallowed into the largest chamber, the rumen, and partly broken down. Later, it is brought back into the mouth and chewed again – "chewing the cud." After the second swallow it passes to the other three chambers and on to the small intestine.

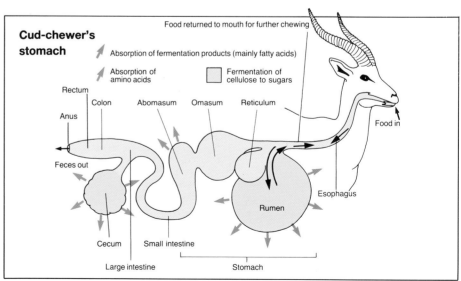

Cud-chewer's stomach

Food returned to mouth for further chewing

Absorption of fermentation products (mainly fatty acids)

Absorption of amino acids

Fermentation of cellulose to sugars

Rectum
Colon
Abomasum
Omasum
Reticulum
Anus
Food in
Feces out
Esophagus
Rumen
Cecum
Small intestine
Large intestine
Stomach

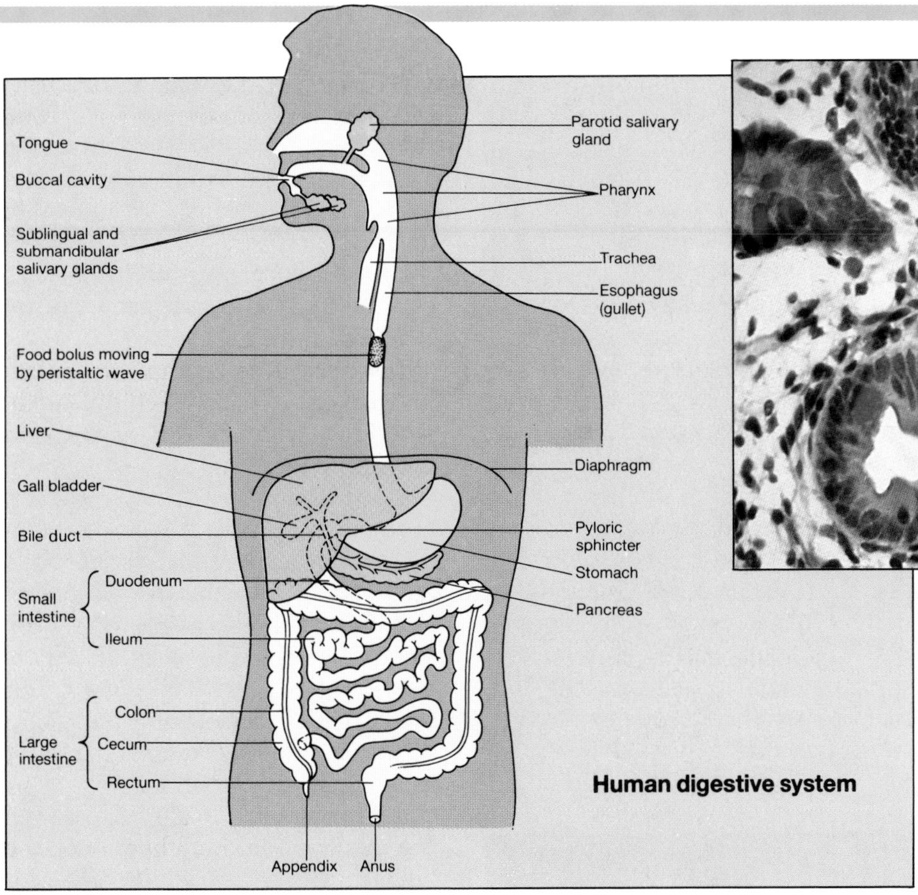
Tongue
Buccal cavity
Sublingual and submandibular salivary glands
Food bolus moving by peristaltic wave
Liver
Gall bladder
Bile duct
Small intestine
Duodenum
Ileum
Large intestine
Colon
Cecum
Rectum
Appendix
Anus
Parotid salivary gland
Pharynx
Trachea
Esophagus (gullet)
Diaphragm
Pyloric sphincter
Stomach
Pancreas
Human digestive system

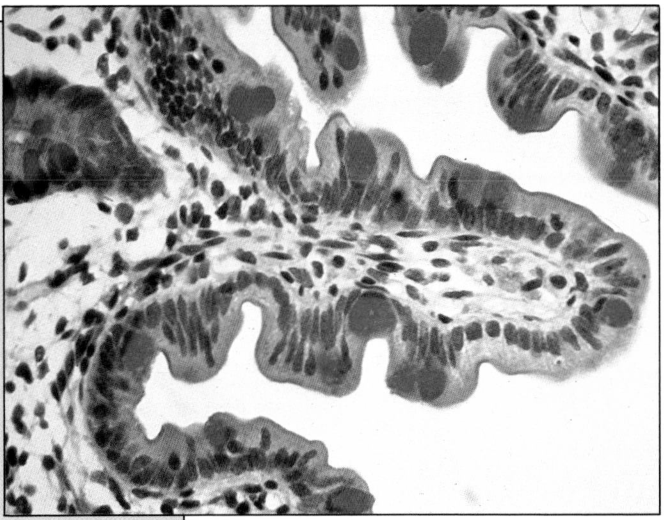

◀▲Our own digestive system is a good example of the mammalian design. It is able to deal with most foods, from meat to tough plants and nuts. The salivary glands produce watery saliva that makes the food mushy, slippery, and easy to swallow. Inside the small intestine, the lining has many small finger-like folds called villi (magnified in the photograph above). These greatly increase the surface area for absorbing food.

In their food and feeding methods, animals are extremely varied. Herbivores, carnivores, fluid-suckers and filter-feeders take in very different kinds of food. But at the level of cells and body chemicals, they are much less varied. So we find that much the same types of digestive enzymes are present throughout the whole of the Animal Kingdom.

BASIC NEEDS

The basic nutrient needs of different animals are also very similar. They require energy sources. They all need proteins (in meat and some plant materials), lipids (in fatty and oily foods), and carbohydrates (starches, sugars and cellulose). They also need small amounts of other substances, such as minerals.

Animals have three main types of enzymes to deal with these nutrients. Carbohydrases split carbohydrates into simpler sugars. Peptidases split proteins into amino acids, and the enzymes called esterases split lipids into fatty acids and glycerol.

ESSENTIAL EXTRAS

Animal enzymes are themselves proteins, but they often have several other chemical substances built into them, which are essential for their working. These extra substances include vitamins and minerals.

For example, in humans, the vitamin folic acid is essential for healthy blood. If it is lacking in food, then the person will become pale, breathless, tired and weak. This condition is known as anemia. A lack of the mineral iron can also be a cause of anemia. Many animals have similar needs for vitamins and minerals.

THE THROUGH-TUBE

The digestive system of an anemone is just a simple bag inside the animal's "stalk." Food is taken into the mouth, digested, and any leftovers are then pushed out of the mouth.

Most other animals have a tube-based digestive system. Food enters the mouth, is digested and absorbed as it moves through the tube. Leftovers and wastes pass out of the other end, the anus. Many worms have this design, where the tube is fairly simple and straight.

In more complex animals, parts of the digestive tube become specialized, and the tube itself is folded and coiled within the body. After the mouth there may be a crop to store food, a gizzard that grinds it up, and a stomach which pulverizes it and bathes it with digestive juices. Then comes the small intestine, which absorbs some of the nutrients. The large intestine absorbs further nutrients, water and minerals. The final part of the system is the rectum. It stores the wastes, called feces, until they are expelled from the body.

CIRCULATION, HEART, BLOOD

In the cold north of Canada, a Snowshoe hare noses for food among patches of frozen snow. As it moves near a clump of bushes, a lynx bursts from the undergrowth and rushes at the hare. But the hare is too quick, and dashes away at great speed. The lynx gives chase for a time, but soon it has to stop, panting heavily and with its heart pounding in its chest.

The processes of life require many substances to be moved from one part of the body to another. Oxygen must be brought to the tissues for respiration. Carbon dioxide is taken away. Nutrients from food must be carried from the digestive system to other parts of the body. There they are stored, or used for their energy value,

or else built into new body tissues. If the distances are sufficiently small, up to about ½in, these movements can happen by diffusion (page 16). Substances simply spread through the body, from areas where they are being produced and their levels are high, to parts where they are being used up.

For example, a flatworm is only about ⅒in thick, although it may be a few inches long. No part of its body is more than ½in from the outside. Oxygen can diffuse in and carbon dioxide can diffuse out fast enough to supply the animal's needs. Also, the flatworm's gut has many fine branches that spread through its body. No part is far from digested nutrients. So flatworms do not need a special system for transporting substances such as food or oxygen around the body. The same is true for many of the smaller kinds of animal.

LONG-DISTANCE TRANSPORT

Most larger animals need to move substances over longer distances. Their bodies are too big for oxygen, carbon dioxide, nutrients and other materials to spread quickly enough by diffusion. So many animals have evolved a circulatory system based on a special fluid – the blood.

The circulatory system is a branching network of tubes known as blood vessels, in which blood goes round and round (circulates).

Blood is a "carrier liquid." It collects nutrients from the digestive system and conveys them to other body parts. Some nutrients are processed and altered in the liver. Others are stored, for example as fat. Some are used for body-building, growth and repair. Energy-containing nutrients are taken to the muscles and used for movement.

In many groups of animals, oxygen is also carried in the blood, from the lungs or gills to the body tissues.

In addition, blood is part of the waste-disposal system. It collects carbon dioxide and wastes from the tissues and takes them to certain organs, such as the kidneys, where they can be eliminated from the animal's body through the urine.

THE HEART OF THE SYSTEM

Blood is pumped around the system by a length of blood vessel which has become thickened, more muscular, and specialized for squeezing. This is the heart. Most animals have one heart. But complex molluscs such as the squid and octopus have three hearts each, and in some kinds of worms, for example earthworms, individuals have five or more pairs. The simplest kind of heart is a tube

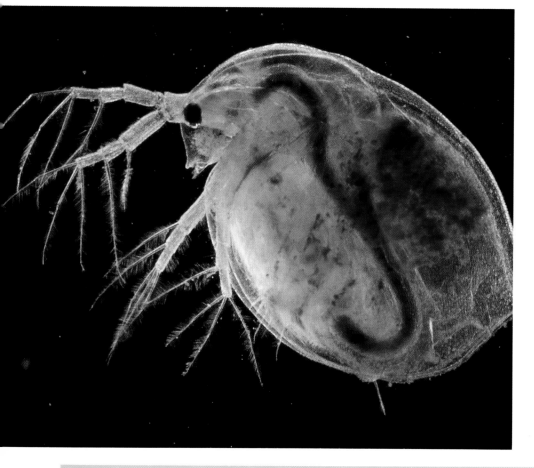

◀The beating heart of the Water flea, *Daphnia*, helps to circulate the "blood" that fills its body. The heart shows through the transparent body. Unlike most crustacean blood, *Daphnia*'s contain the red pigment hemoglobin.

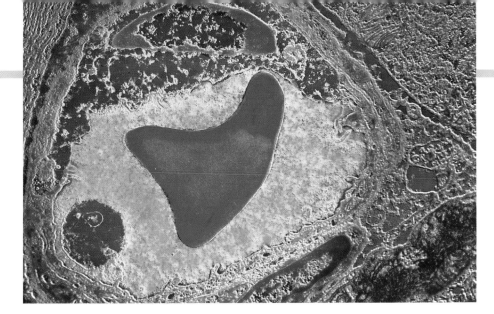

▲ A red blood cell flowing through the smallest of blood vessels, a capillary looks like this under the microscope. In the narrowest capillaries, the tiny red blood cells have to move along in single file, pressed against the capillary walls.

with muscular walls, that pushes blood along by wave-like contractions of the muscles, called peristalsis. Sea squirts (bag-like animals that filter sea water for food) have this type of heart. It can pump blood in either direction. A sea squirt pumps its blood one way for a few minutes, then reverses the direction of pumping and the direction of flow of the blood.

The hearts of other animals pump blood in one direction only. There are non-return valves in the heart, and sometimes in the main blood vessels. These allow blood to pass through one way, but shut to prevent it flowing in reverse.

HOW MANY CHAMBERS?

The hearts of the molluscs (snails, shellfish and their relatives) have two main chambers. These are the atrium, (also called the auricle) and the ventricle. The atrium has thinner, slacker walls than those of the much more muscular ventricle.

Blood returns from the body parts along blood vessels to the atrium. This contracts to squeeze blood into the ventricle. The thick-walled ventricle then contracts more powerfully to push the blood out into the blood

vessels again. Amphibians and reptiles have hearts which have two atria. Blood from both these flows into a single ventricle. This pumps blood to the body and lungs. Birds and mammals have two atria and two ventricles, as part of their double-circulation, explained below.

THE BEAT GOES ON

The heart pumps rhythmically, alternately contracting its muscular walls to push blood out, and then relaxing them as it refills. Each of these cycles of contraction and relaxation is called a heartbeat.

Heartbeats do not happen at a constant speed in all animals. In general, smaller animals have faster heart rates. At rest, a shrew's heart pumps at more than 200 beats per minute. A human heart rate is around 60 to 70 per minute, and an elephant's about 25 per minute.

The warm-blooded birds and mammals have faster heart rates than cold-blooded creatures such as reptiles, because their bodies use up energy faster in making heat.

Heart rate changes according to the activity of the animal. Muscles that are working hard need greater supplies of

▶ Being so tall brings problems for the circulation. The giraffe's heart pumps very strongly to force blood up to its head, 16ft above the ground. When it bends to drink, special valves in the neck veins reduce the blood pressure.

oxygen and energy, so blood flow to them must be increased. The human heart, which is about the size of a clenched fist, pumps some 9 pints of blood each minute when the person is resting. After strenuous exercise it beats much faster and more powerfully, and pumps up to eight times as much blood per minute.

DIVIDING AND DIVIDING

There are three main kinds of blood vessels in the circulatory system: arteries, veins and capillaries. Arteries carry blood away from the heart. Veins bring it back. Capillaries are the smallest and thinnest blood vessels. They link the arteries and veins.

In the arteries, blood is at relatively high pressure as it spurts out of the heart with each beat. In veins, the pressure is much less and the blood oozes along slowly. This is why arteries need thicker walls than veins.

The larger arteries of vertebrates (fish, amphibians, reptiles, birds and mammals) have a substance called elastin in their walls. It is a protein with rubber-like properties. It lets the artery swell with each heartbeat, and then makes it shrink again by elastic recoil. This helps to smooth out the movement of blood, changing any sudden surges into a more even flow.

In many animals the arteries form a branching network, dividing many times and becoming smaller each time. They spread out to all body parts, getting narrower and narrower until they become capillaries.

THE GREAT EXCHANGE

Capillaries are only a fraction of an inch across, and their walls are just one cell thick. The blood inside them is only a very small distance from the surrounding tissues.

At this microscopic level, diffusion works efficiently. In the lungs or gills, oxygen from the air or water diffuses through the lining and across the capillary wall into the blood. In the

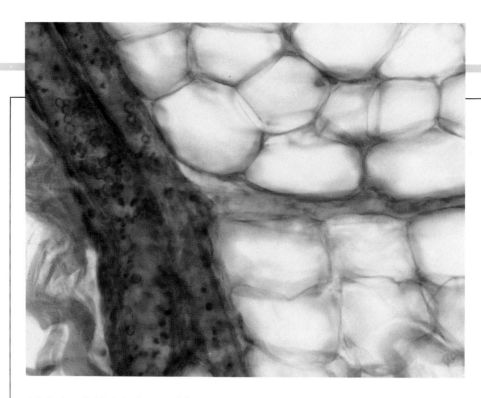

▲Arteries divide into finer and finer vessels as they carry blood into the organs and tissues of the body. The smallest vessels visible here are capillaries running into an area of connective tissue.

Blood vessels
▶Non-return valves in the circulatory system make sure that blood travels in one direction. Blood going the wrong way makes the valve flaps bulge and seal together.

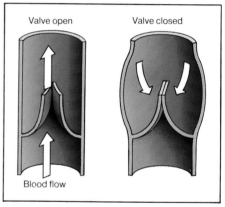

Valve open   Valve closed

Blood flow

▼The three main types of blood vessels. Veins **(1)** carry blood back to the heart. They have a middle layer of muscle and fibers, and a tough outer covering. Arteries **(2)** take blood away from the heart. The thick, muscular middle layer withstands surges in blood pressure with each heartbeat. Capillaries **(3)** are small and thin-walled.

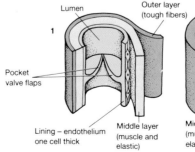

Lumen

Endothelium – one cell thick

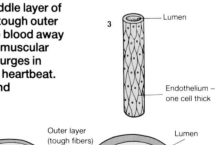

Lumen

Outer layer (tough fibers)

Lumen

Pocket valve flaps

Lining – endothelium one cell thick

Middle layer (muscle and elastic)

Middle layer (muscle and elastic fibers)

Lining-endothelium one cell thick

Outer layer (tough fibers)

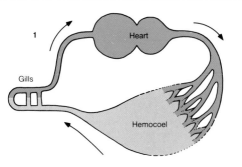

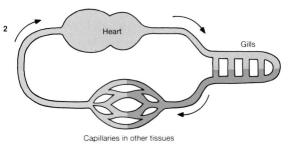

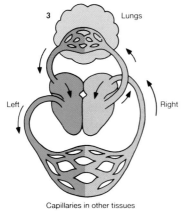

Circulatory systems

Types of blood circulation. In crustaceans (such as crabs) and molluscs (such as squid) **(1)**, blood flows from body tissues into the general body cavity, the hemocoel, and then to the heart through the gills. In fishes **(2)**, the blood passes from the heart to the gills, and then on to other body tissues. In birds and mammals **(3)** the heart is two-sided and there is a double circulation. One side sends blood to the lungs and one to the other body parts.

Capillaries in other tissues

| | Oxygen-rich blood |
| | Oxygen-poor blood |

HEART AND BLOOD CIRCULATORY SYSTEMS

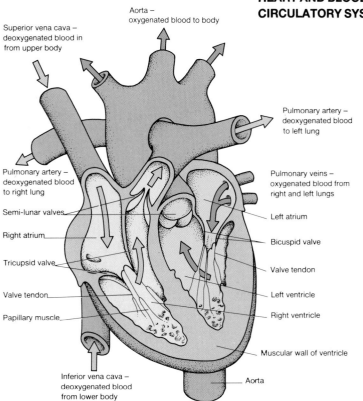

Aorta – oxygenated blood to body

Superior vena cava – deoxygenated blood in from upper body

Pulmonary artery – deoxygenated blood to left lung

Pulmonary veins – oxygenated blood from right and left lungs

Pulmonary artery – deoxygenated blood to right lung

Semi-lunar valves

Right atrium

Tricupsid valve

Valve tendon

Papillary muscle

Left atrium

Bicuspid valve

Valve tendon

Left ventricle

Right ventricle

Muscular wall of ventricle

Inferior vena cava – deoxygenated blood from lower body

Aorta

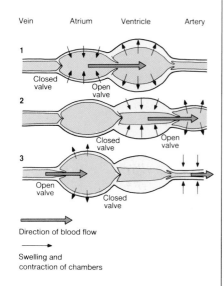

Vein   Atrium   Ventricle   Artery

Closed valve   Open valve

Closed valve   Open valve

Open valve   Closed valve

→ Direction of blood flow

→ Swelling and contraction of chambers

The heart

▲The heart of a mammal, such as a human. It is basically a muscular pump, with two main chambers on each side, an upper atrium and a lower ventricle. The right side (on the left, facing you in the diagram) receives blood from body parts and pumps it to the lungs for fresh oxygen along the pulmonary arteries. The oxygen-rich blood returns to the left side along pulmonary veins.

▲The atrium and ventricle work together to pump blood. The atrium contracts **(1)**, filling the ventricle through the open valve between them. Blood is prevented from going back into the vein by the closed valve on the left. The ventricle's strong muscular walls contract and squeeze blood out into the artery **(2)**, which bulges under the pressure. The valve in the center is now closed, and the one on the right opens. The artery's elastic wall returns to its normal size **(3)**, and the atrium refills from the vein.

digestive system, nutrients diffuse from inside the intestine through its thin lining into the blood.

In the body tissues, oxygen and nutrients diffuse from the blood through the capillary walls and out to the tissues beyond. Carbon dioxide and other wastes diffuse the opposite way, from the tissues into the blood, and are carried off.

Capillaries join together to form larger and larger vessels, eventually becoming veins. The network of veins collects blood from all over the body and brings it back to the heart.

VARIATIONS ON A THEME

Not all animals have the full circulatory system of arteries, capillaries and veins. In some arthropods – such as crabs, lobsters, other crustaceans and spiders – the arteries do not end in capillaries. They open into a blood-filled cavity, the hemocoel, which is the main body cavity of these animals.

Gastropod molluscs (such as snails) and bivalve molluscs (such as mussels and oysters) also have this system. The blood oozes through the hemocoel and is channeled into the gills before

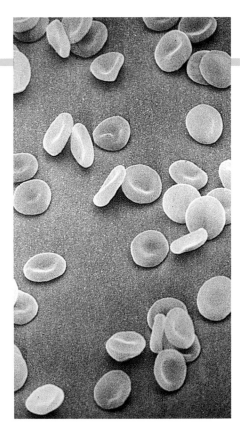

▶Under an electron microscope, red blood cells are revealed as tiny discs with a dimple in each side. (The microscope takes only black-and-white photographs). A human body makes two million new red cells every second.

▼One function of the blood is to clot, to seal breaks and wounds. A series of chemical reactions, started by damage to a blood vessel, forms the string-like substance fibrin. Blood cells are caught in the fibrin net and form a clot.

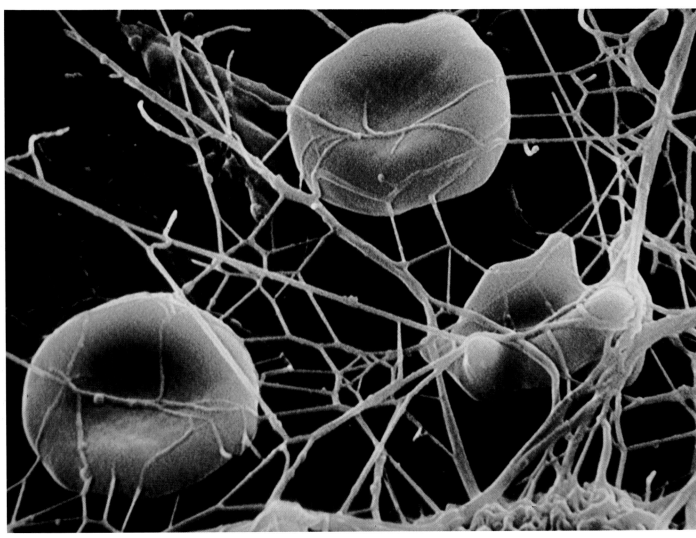

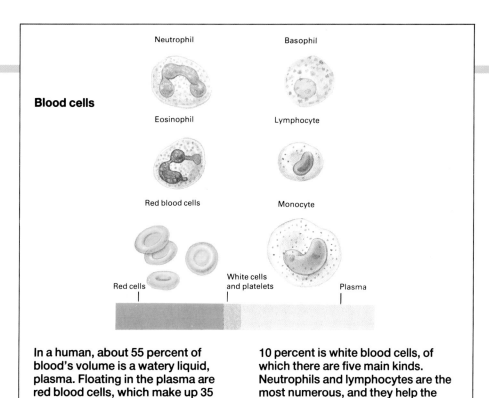

Blood cells

Neutrophil

Basophil

Eosinophil

Lymphocyte

Red blood cells

Monocyte

Red cells

White cells and platelets

Plasma

In a human, about 55 percent of blood's volume is a watery liquid, plasma. Floating in the plasma are red blood cells, which make up 35 percent of the volume. The remaining

10 percent is white blood cells, of which there are five main kinds. Neutrophils and lymphocytes are the most numerous, and they help the body to fight infection by germs.

traveling back to the heart. In insects, the blood circulation simply passes through the heart to the hemocoel and back to the heart. Oxygen travels to the tissues along air-filled tubes, tracheae (page 19), so the blood is not involved in carrying it.

Mammals and birds have a two-sided heart and a double circulation. Blood leaving the right side goes to the lungs, where it takes up oxygen and gets rid of carbon dioxide. It comes back to the left side and is driven out on a second journey, to all the body tissues except the lungs. It then returns to the right side of the heart, and the cycle begins again.

WHY IS OUR BLOOD RED?
Many of the substances that blood carries, such as nutrients and the waste urea, are dissolved in it. It is also carrying some dissolved oxygen. However, in many groups of animals, the bulk of the oxygen is carried in chemical combination with other substances, the blood pigments.

Vertebrates have the blood pigment hemoglobin, which is red in color, and it is this which makes blood red.

Hemoglobin is contained in small doughnut-shaped cells, red blood cells, which float in the blood. In every human red blood cell there are about 270 million hemoglobin molecules, and there are five million red cells in a tiny drop of blood.

Crustaceans and molluscs have a similar blood pigment, hemocyanin, that helps to carry oxygen. But this pigment is light blue.

BLOOD'S OTHER ROLES
Blood is not simply a fetcher and carrier of nutrients. It has many other roles in the body. The white blood cells are part of the immune system which defends the body against invading germs. White cells either "eat" the invaders, or make substances called antibodies that kill or disable them.

Another type of blood cell, the platelet, is involved in the process of blood clotting. This seals cuts and leaks in the body. In warm-blooded animals, blood spreads out heat from the hotter, more active organs such as the muscles and heart, to warm the cooler parts. The continual movement of blood is therefore vital to life.

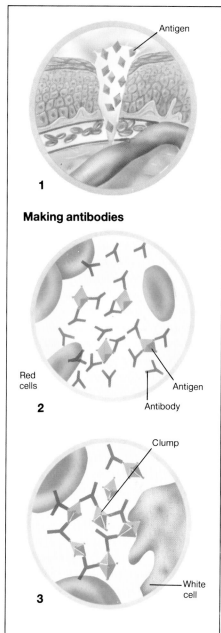

Making antibodies

1

Red cells

Antigen

Antibody

2

Clump

White cell

3

▲ White blood cells attack invading germs in several ways. One method involves making substances called antibodies. Germs, shown by the green diamond shapes, enter the skin through a cut (1). White blood cells release Y-shaped antibodies (2), which are specific for that type of germ. The antibodies stick to the germs and make them burst or clump together. The germs are then eaten by other white cells (3) in the way that amoeba eats its food.

EXCRETION, WATER BALANCE

After a long trek across the desert, the camel looks thin and straggly. It is only two-thirds of its usual body weight. The other third was water which it has lost despite producing only small amounts of very concentrated urine. It has not had a drink for about 10 weeks. At the water hole, it makes up for this – by drinking 35 gallons of water at one session!

The processes of life produce waste substances. Chemicals like urea and ammonia are wastes that come from the breakdown of proteins. Animals need some way of getting rid of these. This is the job of the excretory system.

Small and simple animals can lose wastes from the body by diffusion (page 16). But in larger animals it is not so easy. A variety of excretory systems has evolved. These control both the disposal of wastes and the ins and outs of water balance. In complex animals, the main excretory organs are usually called kidneys.

ADDING AND SUBTRACTING

Although the organs differ, the basic process of excretion is the same across the Animal Kingdom. Body fluids flow into the hollow part of the excretory organ, which is often tube-shaped. As the fluid moves along the tube, cells in the lining absorb water from it. Or, they may add water to the fluid, depending on the animal's water balance at the time. The cells get rid of wastes into the fluid. They can also take in or remove salts, again depending on current needs. Finally the fluid, containing wastes and excess water, leaves the animal as urine.

Sometimes these substances are moved in the opposite way to the way they would go by diffusion. This is because the excretory cells have "pumps," which use energy to force substances from one place to another against the flow of diffusion. So excretion is a process that needs energy, like muscle action.

SUCKING IN THE SEA

Sea water has substances dissolved in it. Most invertebrate animals such as jellyfish and starfish, and some fish such as sharks and rays have body fluids with the same concentration of dissolved substances as sea water, or slightly higher. This means they are in balance with their surroundings, or water tends to flow in very slowly. But the excess water is not too great, and

▶ On the hot, dry African grasslands, a daily trek to the water hole is essential for animals such as this Brindled gnu. It loses water continuously as breathed out moisture from its lungs, and through its skin. Making urine also uses up the body's water supply.

▲ Sea snake

◀ Angel fish

▶ Pigeon

▲▶Animals in different environments face very different problems of water balance. Fish body fluids are less concentrated than sea water, so water tends to pass out through their body walls. To replace this, they drink water and make only small amounts of urine. A sea snake also gradually loses water into the sea, but can get water from the animals it catches, which are less salty than the sea. Seed-eating birds such as pigeons get little water in their food and drink wherever they can. Birds make a paste-like urine.

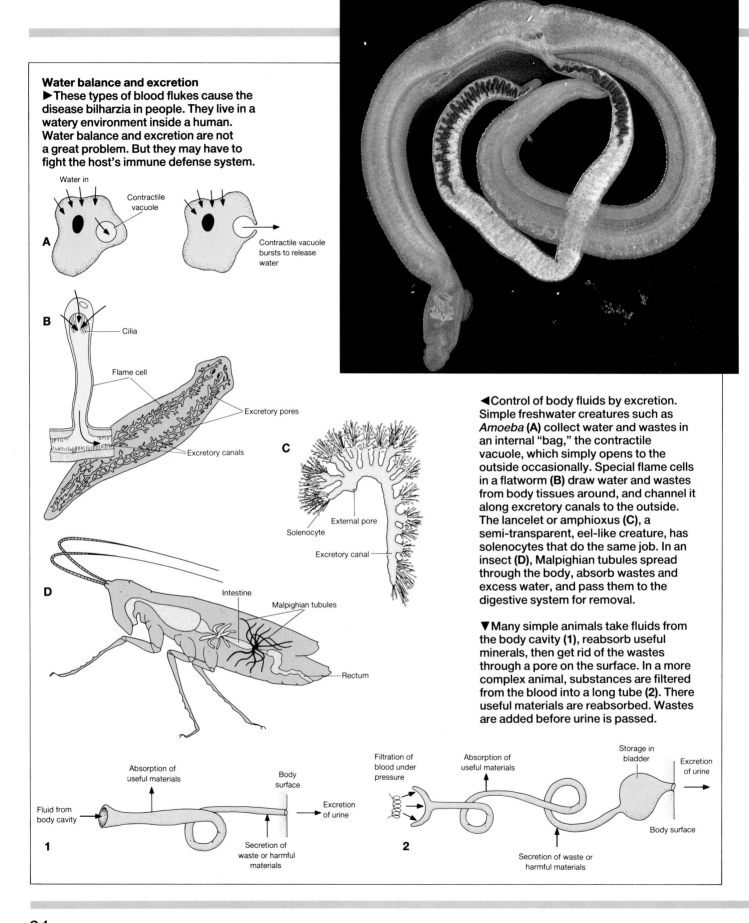

Water balance and excretion
►These types of blood flukes cause the disease bilharzia in people. They live in a watery environment inside a human. Water balance and excretion are not a great problem. But they may have to fight the host's immune defense system.

A
Water in
Contractile vacuole
Contractile vacuole bursts to release water

B
Cilia
Flame cell
Excretory pores
Excretory canals

C
External pore
Solenocyte
Excretory canal

D
Intestine
Malpighian tubules
Rectum

◄Control of body fluids by excretion. Simple freshwater creatures such as *Amoeba* (**A**) collect water and wastes in an internal "bag," the contractile vacuole, which simply opens to the outside occasionally. Special flame cells in a flatworm (**B**) draw water and wastes from body tissues around, and channel it along excretory canals to the outside. The lancelet or amphioxus (**C**), a semi-transparent, eel-like creature, has solenocytes that do the same job. In an insect (**D**), Malpighian tubules spread through the body, absorb wastes and excess water, and pass them to the digestive system for removal.

▼Many simple animals take fluids from the body cavity (**1**), reabsorb useful minerals, then get rid of the wastes through a pore on the surface. In a more complex animal, substances are filtered from the blood into a long tube (**2**). There useful materials are reabsorbed. Wastes are added before urine is passed.

1
Absorption of useful materials
Body surface
Fluid from body cavity
Excretion of urine
Secretion of waste or harmful materials

2
Filtration of blood under pressure
Absorption of useful materials
Storage in bladder
Excretion of urine
Secretion of waste or harmful materials
Body surface

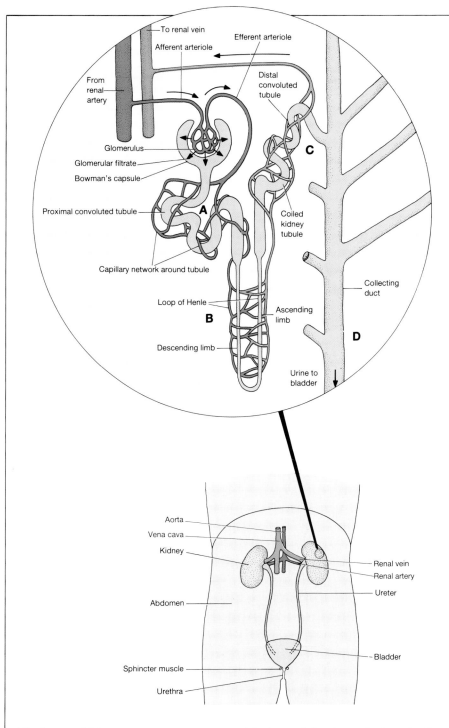

The human kidneys
In each human kidney are 1 million tiny filtering units (above). Blood from the renal artery flows through a knot of capillaries, the glomerulus. Many substances are filtered from this into the tubule (**A**). Farther along the tubule, useful water and mineral salts are taken back into the blood (**B** and **C**). The resulting fluid, urine, flows into a collecting duct (**D**). Many ducts in each kidney come together at its center, and urine trickles down the ureter into the bladder.

the excretory organs such as kidneys can cope with the rate of inflow.

DRINKING THE SEA
A second main group of sea creatures includes crabs and other crustaceans, and most kinds of fish. Their body fluids are less concentrated than sea water. So water tends to be lost from their bodies.

These animals obtain extra water from three sources. One is water in food, which is especially important in plant-eaters such as surgeonfish and sea-cows. Another is water obtained from chemical breakdown of food. The third source is sea water that they drink. They quickly get rid of the extra salt they take in, pumping it out through the gills. They lose some salts in their feces, and make very concentrated urine. Water is left, available for body tissues.

Freshwater animals such as worms, crayfish and fish have the opposite problem. Water floods into their bodies from the weaker solution that surrounds them. Their kidneys make large amounts of dilute urine. This gets rid of wastes and extra water.

HIDING FROM THE SUN
On land, animals dispose of body wastes in urine, along with some water. They also lose water in breathed-out air, and as sweat.

Many are able to control their waste and water loss by behavior. For example, desert-dwellers such as gerbils stay in the cool shade during the day. They also make extremely small amounts of concentrated urine, and use little water in their feces. Several kinds of desert insects can absorb water vapor in the air through their body coverings.

Some creatures get all their water supplies from food. Mosquitoes and leeches have plenty of water in the blood they suck. Mountain gorillas eat large quantities of succulent leafy plants, and rarely need to drink.

KEEPING CONSTANT

In the cool morning, just after sunrise, a group of Australian children walk to their outback school. As they pass a stony outcrop they disturb a lizard basking on a rock. It waddles slowly for cover. When the children return at midday, the lizard has gone. They wonder: is it hunting for food somewhere, or is it now too hot in the Sun for the lizard?

Single-celled animals live in a wide variety of surroundings, from freezing polar seas to hot-water springs. But they cannot survive in deserts or up in the air. Some multi-celled animals, from tiny insects to mighty eagles, can live in such places. In multi-celled animals, different parts of the body can have specialized functions. This means that each one of the many different types of body cells does not have to be adapted to withstand extremes of temperature, dryness and other difficult conditions. Instead, the cells can be adapted to do their jobs and work together, to make the whole body more efficient. Multi-celled animals may live in amazingly varied surroundings, but keep conditions inside their bodies much the same. This process of keeping internal conditions of the body constant is known as homeostasis.

BODY HOUSEKEEPING
The body cells of most animals are about 60 to 80 percent water. Most have fairly similar concentrations of dissolved substances. The temperature at which the cells can live ranges from about 32°F to 110°F.

Yet animals exist in surroundings which differ greatly from these internal conditions. One example is living out of water. A land animal must have a fairly waterproof skin to keep in body fluids. It must also take in water regularly, to replace the water lost.

Also, an animal has to keep up the supply of nutrients to its cells and must get rid of wastes before these build up and become poisonous. All these processes are examples of ways in which the body's internal environment is regulated.

HEAT FROM OUTSIDE
Another example of homeostasis is the way that some animals control their body temperature, so that they neither overheat their body cells nor freeze them to death. Almost all animals depend on warmth coming from their surroundings to maintain their body temperature. They are often called "cold-blooded," but this is not a very accurate term. On a hot day a "cold-blooded" desert snake may be much warmer than the "warm-blooded" jerboa it catches. A more accurate term is *ectothermic*, which means "heat from without."

Creatures that cannot move about, such as barnacles and mussels, must withstand a wide range of temperatures, as the hot Sun shines down and then cold waves cover them a minute later. Their shells help to protect them from these extremes, as well as from the drying effects of Sun and wind.

SUNBATHING IN THE SHADE
Of the ectothermic creatures that can move about, many are able to control their body temperature by their behavior. Scarab beetles and horned lizards are especially good at this. Their behavior is adapted to finding places which are warm when their bodies are too cold, and then locating cool places if they become too hot. These types of animal often follow a

◀Some creatures that live through freezing conditions, like fish in polar seas, and this hibernating Peacock butterfly, have special "antifreeze" chemicals in their blood and body fluids.

▲As winter approaches, the Arctic hare grows a thick white coat of fur. This not only keeps it warm in the bitter cold, but also makes it hard to see against the white snowy background.

▼As the temperature drops to 35°F below freezing, Gentoo penguins endure an Antarctic snowstorm. They keep the body center warm and the outer parts, like feet, just above freezing.

▶The penguin's flippers and feet have a heat-exchanging system. Warm blood from the body center passes heat to the cold blood returning from the limb. Along the limb temperatures drop.

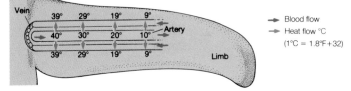

Vein | 39° | 29° | 19° | 9° | Artery
40° | 30° | 20° | 10°
39° | 29° | 19° | 9° | Limb

➡ Blood flow
➡ Heat flow °C
(1°C = 1.8°F+32)

daily routine. At night they shelter in or near large trees, rocks and other places that have absorbed the Sun's warmth during the day. The warmth is given out slowly during the cool night.

At dawn, they come out to bask in the Sun's rays and warm up their bodies, ready for activities such as feeding or nest-building. During the midday heat, they shelter in the shade, often where there is a breeze. At dusk they sunbathe once again, to absorb as much warmth as possible before night begins again.

WARMTH FROM WITHIN

A few groups of animals can regulate their body temperature using heat generated within the body by its own chemical processes. These animals are called *endothermic*. The two main endo-thermic groups are mammals and birds. A few insects such as bees and moths are also able to warm them-selves from within.

Most mammals maintain their body temperature at about 98°F. Most birds function at about 102°F. To keep this internal temperature constant while the temperature outside varies, they need to adjust the amount of heat made or lost from their bodies.

Since the ectotherm's body tends to be warmer than the surroundings, controlling heat loss is important. Mammals have fur and an insulating layer of fat under the skin, while birds have feathers to keep heat in. In the cold, they fluff up the fur or feathers so that they trap more air and improve insulation. Muscles may also "shiver," creating more heat.

◀Northern elephant seals bask on a beach off the coast of California. The Sun could cause overheating and sunburn. These seals have thrown a layer of sand over their backs. The light-colored sand reflects the Sun's rays and keeps the animals cool and safe from sunburn. Sunbathing is often a useful way of conserving body warmth, and therefore saving energy.

KEEPING COOL

Animals cool themselves in several ways. Blood vessels near the surface widen to lose extra heat. Sweat evaporates from the skin. Fluids can evaporate from the mouth and breathing airways. This is what happens when a dog pants.

Endothermic creatures that live in cold seas, such as whales and seals, do not try to keep the whole of the body warm. They have a network of blood vessels at the base of each limb that acts as a heat-exchanger. This helps keep the heat in the body center.

▶Any small patch of shade is welcome in the heat of the African Sun. This cheetah family rests under the shadow of a small tree, their mouths open and panting to lose body warmth.

▼After a morning in the blazing Australian Sun, this Perentie monitor lizard has become too hot for comfort, and is cooling off in the shade of a fallen tree trunk.

SENSES

In the fall, two scuba-diving scientists swim in shallow water off the east coast of North America. Rounding a rock, they see the astonishing sight for which they have come. Hundreds of Spiny lobsters are walking purposefully in single file along the sandy bottom, heading for deeper water. How do they know where they are heading? This is what the scientists wish to study.

Animals obtain information about their surroundings using their senses. These detect danger, food, shelter, mates and the other essentials of life. The Spiny lobsters use their sensory information to know when and in which direction to migrate to remain in favorable conditions.

Our own senses are dominated by sight (see page 44). We also use our hearing (page 50) extensively, the sense of touch on our skin (page 54), and taste and smell (page 56). These senses are dealt with on the relevant pages. There are other kinds of senses in the animal world, some of which are described here.

A WORLD OF SENSES

Senses detect many aspects of the outside world. Sight detects light rays. Smell and taste register airborne or waterborne chemicals. Hearing interprets vibrations in air or water. Touch detects physical pressure.

But other senses can detect many other features of the world around an animal. These include the pull of gravity, the speed and direction of movements, the weak lines of magnetic force around the Earth, currents in air and water, humidity, temperature, and electrical signals generated by muscles and other living tissues.

We should be aware that other animals "see" the world in some very

▲ This Common cuttlefish has just caught a Common prawn. It hunted it using its large and sensitive eyes. Once it holds the prey, it receives more sensory information from touch detectors on its tentacles.

▼ This pit viper shows the heat-sensitive pit in front of each eye. Inside the pit is a membrane which detects temperature differences of just 0.01°F and is used to hunt warm-blooded prey. A mouse can be found in total darkness.

different ways to ourselves – perhaps as a complex pattern of water currents and magnetic forces, or as a kaleidoscope of smells.

In complex animals, sensing is the function of receptor cells. These are specialized to detect an aspect of the outside world, change it into tiny electrical nerve signals, and send these signals along nerves to the brain. Sensory cells may be single and scattered in the body, or grouped into specialized parts called sense organs.

TALKING DRUM
Our ears detect airborne vibrations, but vibrations occur in water and in solid objects too. Fish have lateral lines that tell them of vibrations and currents in the water (page 55).

In certain types of spiders that live on banana plants, the male uses vibrations to find his mate. When he detects the scent of a female, he shakes his body and legs. The vibrations pass through the plant to the female, who gives an answering shake. The male then follows the vibrations to find his partner.

ANIMAL COMPASSES
We have invented the magnetic compass to show the direction of the weak lines of magnetic force around the Earth. But experiments have shown that many animals have a magnetic sense – a sort of built-in compass. They include dolphins, birds, mice, snails, bees, butterflies and moths. Many animal migrators navigate at least partly by this magnetic sense.

Scientists do not yet know how the magnetic sense works. They have

▲ The chimaera or ratfish, which is a relative of the sharks, lives deep down in cold seas. The skin on the head, and especially on the rostrum (the "nose" part), is covered with chemical and electrical sensors. Perhaps the ratfish uses these to find prey or breeding partners, in the darkness of the vast ocean depths.

discovered small particles of magnetic material in the skull and neck muscles of birds such as pigeons, which are well-known for their homing abilities. Studies have also shown that some birds use the Sun as a compass pointer on long flights, and that the bird must first "set" the Sun compass using the magnetic compass, before it can use the Sun's direction for navigation.

Among butterflies, the Monarch has the most magnetic particles in its body. This long-distance flier migrates from North America to winter in Mexico. A body compass presumably helps it to find the way as it flies hundreds of miles southwards.

ELECTRIFYING SENSES

A sense which is very important to some fish was discovered in 1951.

Fish such as elephant-snout fish and knifefish produce a continual discharge of electrical pulses from specialized muscles near the tail. These travel through the water and are detected by electrical sensors near the head, which have evolved from part of the lateral line (page 55). Any objects in the water change the pattern of pulses, and the fish senses this. These fish live in murky water. They use their electrical sense for navigation. They can detect plants, riverbanks and other animals up to 3ft away.

Other fish, particularly sharks and rays, have electricity sensors on their skin, but do not produce electrical pulses themselves. They can pick up the weak electrical signals of other animals. Rays detect flatfish buried in the sand, picking up signals from the muscles around the gills of their prey.

Yet other fish, the electric eels and rays, have massive electrical organs that produce shocks of 500 volts or more, to stun their victims (page 55).

CHECKING FOR CHANGES

One feature of sense organs is their ability to stop responding when the same stimulus keeps occurring. It is said: "We cannot afford to feel our socks on our feet all day long." This means that when a sense first detects something, we become aware of it and consider whether we need to take any action. But if the stimulus is of no real importance, the sense organ and brain gradually "ignore" it. Only if it changes, do we take notice again. Our senses, and those of other animals, respond mainly to change.

▲The Emperor tamarin, like other monkeys, relies greatly on its sense of balance while leaping about the forest trees overhanging the River Amazon. It uses its long, furry tail as a counterweight while balancing, and as a steering rudder when jumping.

◄Migrating geese fly in family groups, so the young have the benefit of older geese to guide them along the route. Even so, they can still find their way by instinct alone. They may navigate by the Sun, Moon and stars, and by detecting the Earth's magnetic field.

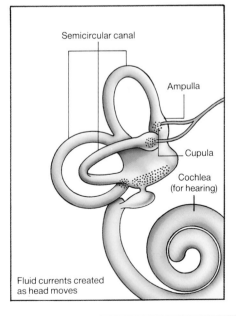

Semicircular canal

Ampulla

Cupula

Cochlea (for hearing)

Fluid currents created as head moves

◄Mammals such as tamarins and humans have balance organs inside the ear. These are three curved tubes, semicircular canals. The canals contain a fluid that swishes round as the head moves. The fluid bends a jelly-like lump, the cupula, in the bulge (ampulla) at the end of the canal. Sensitive hairs embedded in the cupula create nerve signals when they are bent, which are sent to the brain. There is one canal in each dimension (up-down, front-back, left-right), so however the head moves, the fluid flows in at least one of them.

SEEING

In the far north of Scandinavia, a Snowy owl peers into the gathering gloom over the marsh. Unusually for an owl, it hunts mainly by day, although its great eyes can still pick out prey even in the failing light. Spotting a lemming on the far side of the clearing, it swoops down on silent wings. The lemming's poorer vision did not see the owl coming ...

Of all senses, vision is the most valuable for finding out about objects in the landscape. An animal with keen eyes can spot danger far away, so that it has time to escape. Senses such as taste and touch would work too late to avoid the danger.

Sight dominates our own lives so much that we think of the views we see with our eyes as the "real world." It is estimated that four-fifths of the information in the human brain came in via the eyes. A large part of our brain is devoted to analyzing and interpreting what the eyes see.

However, our eyes are only one of many types in the Animal Kingdom. Creatures with other types of eyes may have a very different view of the world. Also, we should remember that many other creatures rely less on vision and more on other senses such as smell or hearing.

EYE AND BRAIN

Animals make use of their eyesight in many ways. Even the simplest eye, which detects only light or dark, can help its owner to select more suitable surroundings. Scallops and fan-worms, with several small simple eyes, use them to detect movements nearby. These can give warning of an approaching predator.

Other eyes form an image of the scene before them, in the form of a two-dimensional "picture." What the animal does with this information depends not on its eyes but on its brain. By itself, an eye is of little use.

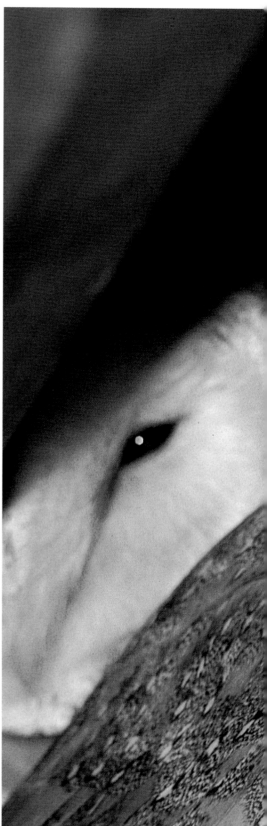

▶ A large part of an owl's head is taken up with its enormous eyes. Active mostly at night, an owl needs eyes which can gather as much light as possible, so it can see to hunt its prey.

▼ The deep-sea Viper fish lives where light seldom penetrates, and meals are few and far between. Its huge eyes collect what light there is, and its long fangs do the same for prey.

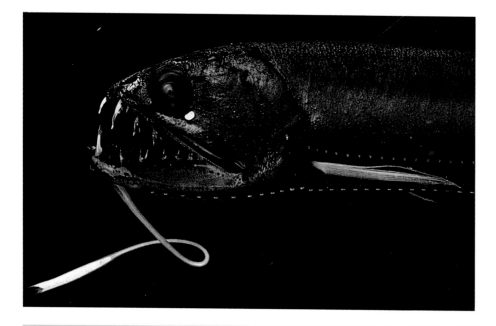

The brain must be able to process what the eyes see and then act on the information they provide.

FROM LIGHT TO ELECTRICITY

The essential part of any eye is the light-sensitive receptor cell. This cell generates nerve signals when light rays fall on it. An example is the rod cell, one type of light receptor cell in the mammal eye.

The rod cell contains a substance which is called visual pigment. This changes its structure when struck by light, which is a form of energy. The energy in the light ray changes the pigment into a more "excited" form. This sets off a series of chemical changes that affect the cell's membrane, closing some channels in the membrane which are usually open when there is no light.

As the channels close, they prevent other electrically-charged substances (mineral ions) from passing into or out of the cell. An imbalance soon builds up, in the form of an electrical charge. This is the beginning of the electrical nerve signal, which flashes along the nerve fiber towards the brain (page 66).

The eye has done its job: light has been turned into nerve signals. The whole process is completed in just a fraction of a second, and the visual pigment reverts to its original state and awaits more light rays. Without this quick recovery an eye would have very limited use.

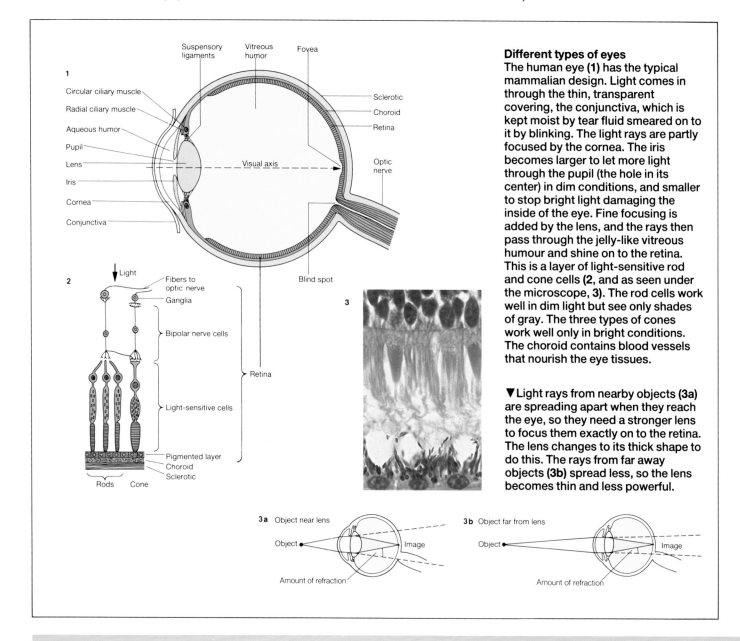

1
- Suspensory ligaments
- Vitreous humor
- Fovea
- Circular ciliary muscle
- Radial ciliary muscle
- Aqueous humor
- Pupil
- Lens
- Iris
- Cornea
- Conjunctiva
- Sclerotic
- Choroid
- Retina
- Visual axis
- Optic nerve
- Blind spot

2
- Light
- Fibers to optic nerve
- Ganglia
- Bipolar nerve cells
- Retina
- Light-sensitive cells
- Pigmented layer
- Choroid
- Sclerotic
- Rods
- Cone

3

Different types of eyes
The human eye **(1)** has the typical mammalian design. Light comes in through the thin, transparent covering, the conjunctiva, which is kept moist by tear fluid smeared on to it by blinking. The light rays are partly focused by the cornea. The iris becomes larger to let more light through the pupil (the hole in its center) in dim conditions, and smaller to stop bright light damaging the inside of the eye. Fine focusing is added by the lens, and the rays then pass through the jelly-like vitreous humour and shine on to the retina. This is a layer of light-sensitive rod and cone cells **(2**, and as seen under the microscope, **3)**. The rod cells work well in dim light but see only shades of gray. The three types of cones work well only in bright conditions. The choroid contains blood vessels that nourish the eye tissues.

▼Light rays from nearby objects **(3a)** are spreading apart when they reach the eye, so they need a stronger lens to focus them exactly on to the retina. The lens changes to its thick shape to do this. The rays from far away objects **(3b)** spread less, so the lens becomes thin and less powerful.

3a Object near lens
- Object
- Image
- Amount of refraction

3b Object far from lens
- Object
- Image
- Amount of refraction

SIMPLE ANIMALS, SIMPLE EYES

A layer of light receptor cells packed closely together is known as a retina. In the course of evolution, about eight different ways have been tried of arranging the retina and other eye parts to produce an image.

The simpler animals, such as flatworms and earthworms, have simple types of eyes. These have a retina that lines a cup-shaped chamber of black pigment in the skin. When light comes from one direction, the pigment cup casts a shadow over the retina on that side. So a very simple image is formed by shadowing, as in a pinhole camera.

A variation on this design is to place each light receptor at the bottom of its own cup or tube. Eyes of this pattern are found in several species of fanworm and tube worm.

LOOKING THROUGH LENSES

Eyes with lenses have evolved many times. The eye lens works like a camera lens, to bend light rays and bring them into sharp focus on the retina. Without a lens the retina just sees a multi-colored blur. Several animal groups have evolved separately eyes comprising a single chamber with a lens inside to focus light on the retina. These include fish, cephalopod molluscs such as the octopus and cuttlefish, gastropod molluscs like conchs, and some types of worms found in the sea.

EXTRA BENDING POWER

In water, light rays bend little as they pass from water to the watery fluid inside the eye. To focus an image on the back of the eye, a fish needs a powerful spherical lens.

Out of water, light rays bend a lot as they go from air to the watery fluid in the eye. Most of the bending in the eyes of land animals takes place at the cornea. This is the curved, transparent "window" at the front of the eye. The lens then adds fine-focusing adjustments, and may be much thinner than the lens in the eye of a water animal such as a fish.

This type of eye is found in the amphibians, reptiles, birds and mammals, and also in spiders. Some kinds

▼Animals whose eyes face forwards, like this Red fox, see a similar scene in each eye – although from slightly different angles. The brain compares the two views and works out the distances of objects. This is called binocular vision. Binocular vision is especially important for hunters as it helps them judge the distance when pouncing on prey.

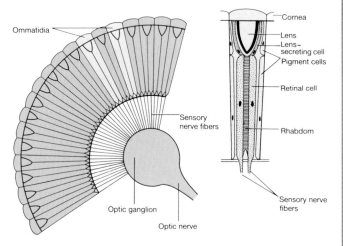

Insect eyes

◄Each of the horsefly's eyes is made of hundreds of separate units, called ommatidia. They see a mosaic-like view of the world. The eyes of the dragonflies can contain up to 30,000 units and give these hunters sharp vision to help find prey.

▲An insect eye with one ommatidium enlarged. The lens carries out some focusing, and the retinal cells in the cone-shaped tube detect the light rays. Nerve fibers run from these to the optic ganglion, and then down the optic nerve to the insect's brain.

of jumping spider, which hunt by sight, have vision almost as good as that of monkeys.

MANY EYES MAKE LIGHT WORK?
In contrast to the single-chambered eye of vertebrates some animals have compound eyes. In these there are many separate units. Each has a lens or other focusing system, and retinal cells that turn the light rays into nerve signals. Compound eyes occur mainly in insects and crustaceans.

A bee's eye has about 5,000 of these separate optical units, called ommatidia. They fit snugly together like the hexagonal cells of a honeycomb. The two compound eyes can see almost all around the bee. The compound eye probably forms a mosaic type of image, although we cannot be

sure how the nerve signals are interpreted in the animal's brain. However, calculations show that a bee's vision is, at best, 60 times less detailed than our own.

A variation on the compound eye is the superposition eye. It is found in night-time insects and deep-sea crustaceans, which live with very low light levels. The individual lenses or mirrors do not each form a separate image, but send their light rays on to the retina lying below. The combined image is considerably brighter than individual ones would be.

WHO CAN SEE COLORS?
Light rays of different colors have different wavelengths. Those with longer wavelengths are red, progressing through the other colors of the

spectrum (the "rainbow") to the violet of the shorter wavelengths of light.

Our eyes have two main kinds of light receptor cells – rods and cones. In each eye there are about 120 million rods and 7 million cones. We have three types of cones. Each type is most sensitive to light of a certain wavelength, depending on the type of visual pigment it contains. Our three cone types pick up mainly blue, green or yellow light. The other colors we see are mixtures of these three.

Many other animals can see in color. The eyes of gorillas and of baboons have the same three visual pigments as us. Frogs have good color vision and are especially sensitive to blue light.

Squirrels and dogs have only two types of visual pigment, so the colors they see may not be as varied as those we can detect. Birds have five types of pigments, and also a filtering system based on droplets of oil in the cone cells, so they can probably distinguish many more colors than us. As scientists continue their research, they are discovering that more and more animals can see colors in one form or another.

SEEING INVISIBLE LIGHT

The shortest wavelength of light that we can see is violet. Yet some insects can see even shorter wavelengths – that is, light which is invisible to the human eye. This is called ultra-violet light. Many flowers have markings that we cannot see, but which bees can see and use to identify the flower and guide them to the source of nectar at a petal's base.

The longest wavelengths we can detect are red. Again some creatures, such as butterflies and snakes, can see light of even longer wavelengths, known as infra-red. Warm objects give off infra-red rays, which are sometimes called "heat waves." Snakes such as pit vipers and rattlesnakes have infra-red detectors in pits on either side of the head, in front of their real eyes. The detectors pick up infra-red rays coming from warmblooded prey such as mice. These snakes can judge the direction and distance of their prey, and strike with deadly accuracy – even in what looks to us like complete darkness.

Light waves can vibrate in different directions, but to our eyes these differences (of "polarization") are not apparent. Some animals, including insects such as bees, have their light-receiving apparatus ordered in a such a way that they see light differently according to which way it is polarized. The pattern of polarization of light from the sky can indicate the Sun's direction even when it is behind cloud. So bees can often "see" the Sun when we cannot.

WHOSE EYES ARE BEST?

Because eyes are specialized for different roles it is hard to say which is best, but birds of prey may see things clearly six times as far away as us. Owls see when it seems pitch black to us.

The size of an eye gives a rough indication of how sharp its owner's vision is likely to be. Ostriches have the largest eyes among all the land animals. The largest eyes of all are the Giant squid's. These can be up to 16in across, and allows the animal to catch prey such as fish and smaller squid deep in the sea.

▼The angwantibo's eyes shine in the African night, reflecting the photographer's flash. This animal has a reflecting layer, or tapetum, behind the retina, which sends light back through the sensitive rod cells, giving a second chance of making use of it.

▲A lioness and cub seen at night with the aid of an image intensifier. This magnifies each photon of light to levels that the human eye can see. There is obviously enough light at night to see clearly if eyes are sufficiently sensitive, like those of many nocturnal animals.

HEARING

Sitting in their country garden on a summer evening, the family talk quietly about plans for the next day. Suddenly the youngest child hears very high-pitched squeaks from nearby. The older child thinks she can hear something, but the parents cannot detect any such sounds. Then a bat flits over the hedge. They realize that the squeaks are being made by this tiny mammal.

Not all ears hear the same sounds. In humans, a young child is able to hear much higher-pitched sounds than older people. The ear's sensitivity to high notes falls with age.

Other animals hear sounds that are much higher, or lower, or quieter, than we can detect. Small mammals like shrews communicate by a range of very high-pitched whistles and pips. Birds such as pigeons may hear some extremely low-pitched noises such as stormy seas throwing waves on the shore.

Sounds too high-pitched for us to detect are known as ultrasound. Those that are too low-pitched we call infrasound. Air, water and solid substances like rocks all carry these sound vibrations. For some animals, sound is the main sense. They "hear" the world in the way we "see" it.

PICKING UP VIBRATIONS
Hearing organs such as ears are specialized to detect vibrations. In air, the vibrations are in the form of sound waves – air molecules moving to and fro at great speed. In water too sound travels through the vibrations of the water molecules. Sound travels even better in water than in air.

These vibrations are a form of energy. The hearing organ changes them into a different form of energy, electrical nerve impulses, which are interpreted in the brain.

USEFULLY DEAF
Surprisingly, some creatures that are otherwise well equipped with sensory organs, such as octopus and squid, lack true ears. However, this may be useful. Some of their main predators are toothed whales such as the Sperm whale, which are thought to stun their prey with incredibly loud bursts of sound. No squid could escape such a powerful noise at close range, but deafness may protect it while the predator is some way off, and let the squid escape.

▶A Red-eyed tree frog blows up its vocal sac as it croaks to other frogs nearby. It then listens with its ears, the green discs just behind the eyes. A frog's hearing is mainly limited to the calls of other frogs of its own kind. It cannot hear many other sounds.

▼Red howler monkeys use sound as a form of communication in their South American tropical forest home. It is difficult to see other members of their group or rival groups among the trees. So the regular dawn chorus of howls lets each monkey know the whereabouts of other howlers more than 1mi away.

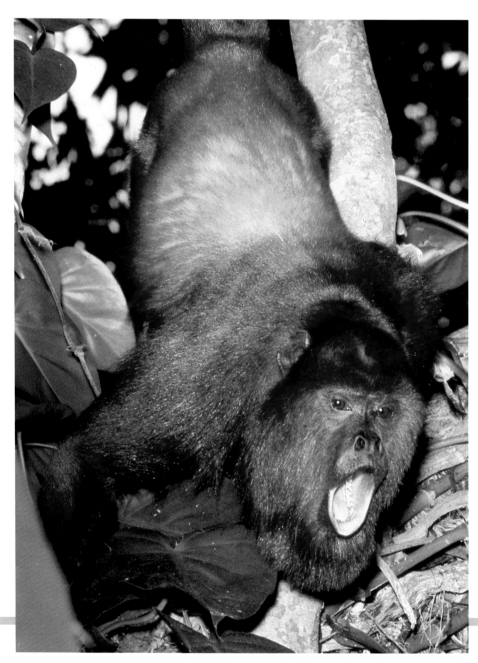

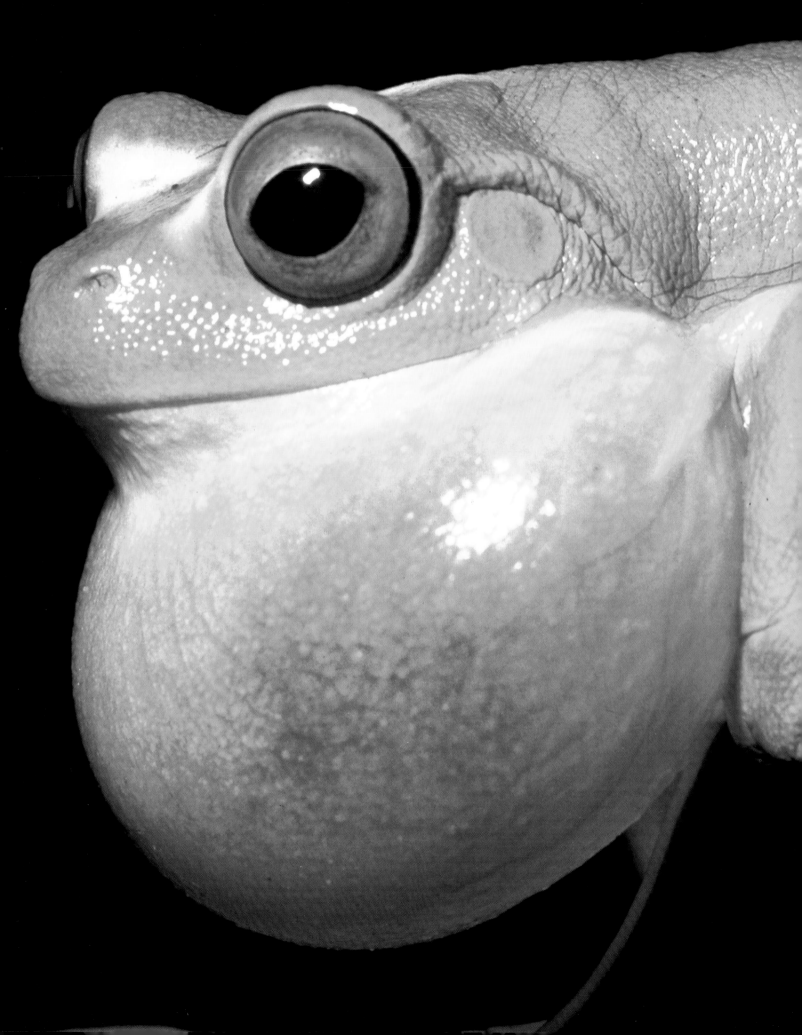

INSIDE AN EAR

Hair cells are the basis of many sensory organs, such as those of balance (page 43). The most intricate use of hair cells is in the mammalian inner ear, in the cochlea.

In mammals, sound waves are collected by the pinna, or ear flap – what we usually call "the ear." Our own pinna is not particularly good at funneling sound waves into the ear, but that of a horse or rabbit is much better, and it can be swiveled to pinpoint the direction of a noise.

Sound waves travel along the ear canal and bounce off the ear drum, making it vibrate. These vibrations are transmitted through the middle ear cavity by three small bones (ossicles) to another membrane, the oval window, which is the entrance to the cochlea itself. The vibrations pass through the window into the fluid within the cochlea.

SNAIL-SHAPE CANAL

The cochlea has the coiled shape of a snail shell. But, to understand its workings, imagine it uncoiled becoming a long, cone-shaped tube. Inside it is a stretched sheet, the basilar membrane. This is the part that enables

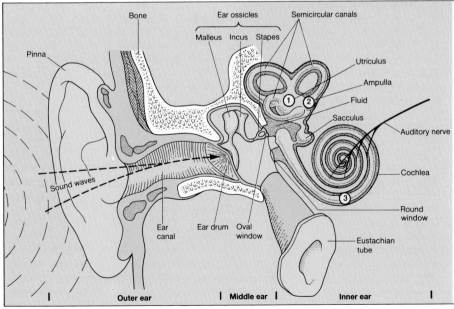

The human ear
◀The human ear senses sounds. It also detects movements of the head and helps keep the balance. Inside the middle ear, sound waves are converted into vibrations of the ear drum, then vibrations of the tiny bones known as ear ossicles, and then vibrations in the fluid of the cochlea, where they are changed into nerve signals. The three numbered circles show the main sensory area. Gravity detection takes place in the utriculus, or utricle (**1**), where tiny hairs (cilia) register movements of a tiny stone (otolith), sideways head movement is detected in the ampulla of the semicircular canals (**2**, and page 43), and sound is registered by the cochlea itself (**3**), shown here in side-on view.

◀A Greater horseshoe bat swoops on a moth, having homed in on it by a "sonar" system of high-pitched sound pulses. The battle is not one-sided, since some moths have listening membranes that hear the pulses, giving time to escape.

▲Sound waves made by whales travel through the oceans for hundreds of miles. The whale makes its eerie "song" by moving air from one part of its body to another. This is a Humpback whale mother and calf.

mammals to detect the pitch, or frequency, of sounds so well.

Hair cells are in contact with the basilar membrane along its length. At the end nearest the oval window, the membrane is quite wide and vibrates best to low frequencies such as a bass drum. At the far end it is narrow and vibrates most strongly to high frequencies, as from a flute.

When sound of a certain pitch reaches the cochlea, it causes the strongest vibrations in just one region of the basilar membrane. This stimulates hair cells in that region and generates a particular pattern of nerve signals. From this the brain recognizes the pitch of a sound. Many noises contain sounds of several pitches.

SONAR HUNTER

Bats use their ears for navigating in the dark. They send out extremely high-pitched clicks, pips and squeaks which are reflected off nearby objects. Their ears detect the returning echoes, and from their pattern, the bat's brain can work out the size of objects and their distance away. They can detect objects as thin as a human hair. A bat uses this echo-location system, which is similar to the sonar "pings" of submarines, to track and catch insects in mid-flight – even in complete darkness.

A few birds, and many whales and dolphins, also listen for the echoes of their own voices, and use them to gather useful information.

CHIRPING AND SINGING

Reptiles, amphibians and fish have simpler ears than mammals. They detect a smaller range of sounds, but can still give useful information to their owners about their own kind. Frogs make many sounds at breeding time, and the sea can be full of fish noises ranging from grunts to a variety of percussion effects. Among the animals without backbones the only really noisy group of animals, with a sense of hearing to match, is the insects. Their only ears are vibrating drum-like membranes with a few receptor cells attached. They are sited on the middle or back part of the body, or on the legs in some grasshoppers.

Most of these simple ears do not have a wide range of pitch. They are tuned into the calls of rivals or mates. The main information in insect song is contained in the pattern of pulses – the way that the sounds start and stop in rapid bursts.

TOUCH

Sitting by the river, the boy sees a fish close to the bank. He creeps forward, trying to stay out of sight. He slowly puts his hand under the surface, to grasp the fish. But as he opens his fingers, he creates a slight ripple in the water – and the fish has gone.

With our fingertips, we can feel vibrations too small for the eye to see. Skin is, in a sense, our biggest sense organ. It detects not only touch but also pressure, heat, cold, and pains caused by extreme heat, crushing pressure, a wound or some other damage.

Receptors that indicate contact with the body surface, which is the basic form of "touch," are found in all

animals. In insects they take the form of bendable hairs, each with one or more sense cells making contact with the base. As in other senses, one form of energy – the energy of movement of the hair – is turned into electrical nerve signals, which are sent along nerves to the brain.

SENSITIVE SKIN

In many other animals, including ourselves, modified nerve endings in the skin, tell us if we have touched something, and also give information on the texture, or feel, of its surface. Each nerve ending has an elastic capsule around it called a corpuscle.

▼**Structure of skin** A step-like cutaway diagram of human skin shows its main layers and the microscopic sensors they contain. These include cold and heat receptors, which are buried quite deeply, and deep pressure receptors which are at the very base of the skin, almost in the fat layer beneath. Light touch receptors, and free nerve endings to sense pain, are near the surface. There are also sensors in the hair root which can feel the hair shaft being pulled or tilted. Skin contains many other structures too, such as blood vessels and sweat glands.

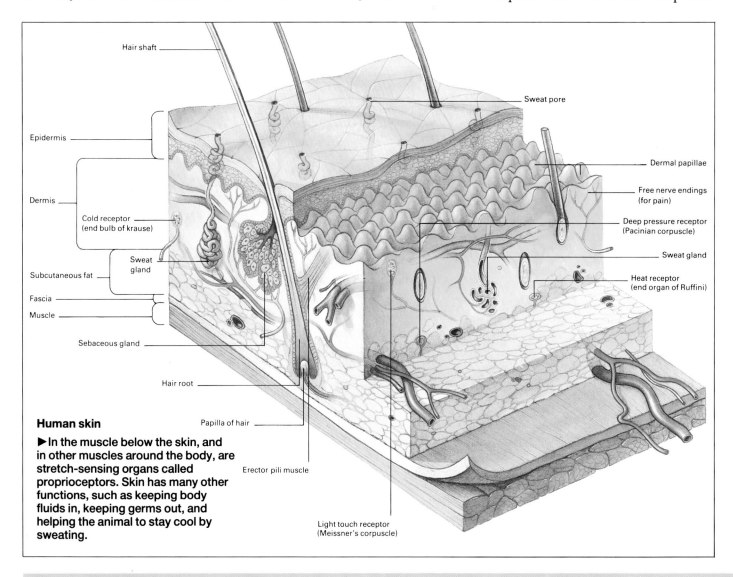

Human skin

▶In the muscle below the skin, and in other muscles around the body, are stretch-sensing organs called proprioceptors. Skin has many other functions, such as keeping body fluids in, keeping germs out, and helping the animal to stay cool by sweating.

Labels: Hair shaft · Sweat pore · Epidermis · Dermal papillae · Free nerve endings (for pain) · Dermis · Cold receptor (end bulb of krause) · Deep pressure receptor (Pacinian corpuscle) · Sweat gland · Sweat gland · Subcutaneous fat · Heat receptor (end organ of Ruffini) · Fascia · Muscle · Sebaceous gland · Hair root · Papilla of hair · Erector pili muscle · Light touch receptor (Meissner's corpuscle)

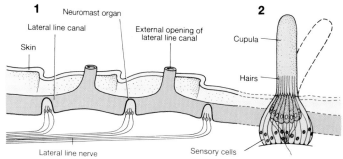

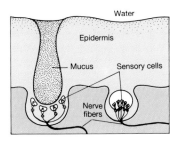

Two types of fish electro-sensors.
▲◄The Electric ray produces massive electrical shocks to stun prey. These are made by specially developed muscles along the body sides. Rays and other fish have electricity sensors in the skin, to detect weak electrical pulses given off by the muscles of other animals. They are good at finding flatfish buried in the sand, and feed on these.

▲(Top) The bleak shows the silvery lateral line on the side of its body. (Above) The lateral line is a groove or tube under the skin (1), with tubular openings to the surface. A single pressure receptor in the line (2). These receptors stick up from the base of the lateral line, as neuromast organs.

It has the effect of transmitting fast events, such as sudden taps which change its shape, to the nerve. But the corpuscle stays bulging out when constant pressure is put on it, and makes few signals. This is why we can no longer really "feel" something in contact with the skin after it has been there for some time, such as the pressure of socks and shoes on our feet (page 43).

INNER FEELINGS

Sensors which detect deformation, or change in shape, are also found in other parts of an animal's body. In the muscles, they measure the stresses (tensions) and the strains (length changes), as the muscles contract and relax when the animal moves. This is known as the proprioceptive sense. It helps the animal to tell the position of the various parts of its body. Muscle length is measured in many animals by elastic, spindle-shaped receptors in the muscle itself. As the muscle is lengthened the receptor is stretched and sends out nerve signals.

Changes in muscle tension are also measured. Insects, with hard, shell-like outer skeletons, usually monitor changes using receptors embedded in the skeleton itself. In mammals, which have an internal bony skeleton, tension is measured in the rope-like tendons that join the muscles to the bones of the body.

DISTANT TOUCH

Water, being much thicker than air, transmits vibrations and ripples well over short distances. Fish can detect these water currents by a type of "touch-at-a-distance" sense organ, the lateral line. In most fish, the lateral line shows as a thin strip along each side of the body, from behind the gill cover to the tail base. The line is a channel, groove or tube under the skin. It has slits or pores opening to the water above. At intervals along the line are clumps of sensory hair cells, with their tips embedded in a jelly-like mass, called the cupula.

Water currents ripple along the lateral line and bend the cupulae. This stimulates the hair cells to make nerve signals. This enables the fish to feel water currents around its body surface, made by the water flowing around rocks and other obstacles or by animals moving nearby.

A modified version of the lateral line sensors is found in the electricity detectors, or electro-sensors, of many fish. These are usually scattered about in the skin, particularly on the head, of fish such as sharks, rays and chimaeras. The electrical "ripples" are focused into a mucus-filled pit and affect the sensory cells there, which pass nerve signals to the brain.

SMELL, TASTE

A kiwi creeps through the dense forest of New Zealand, scratching with its powerful claws and dipping its long beak into the ground, in the search for food. Suddenly it catches the scent of a juicy worm and sticks its beak deep into the leaves, sniffing through its nostrils at the beak's tip. Within a second the prey is located and is on its way down the kiwi's gullet.

Smell and taste are often referred to as the "chemical senses," because they are concerned with detecting certain chemical substances in the animal's surroundings.

Our sense of taste detects the nature of chemicals in the mouth. These are dissolved in water, either in watery fluids already in the food, or released into the watery saliva that we add to food as we chew it. In us, the sense of smell deals mainly with airborne chemicals that float from a distance. They are breathed into the nose and captured by the smell organs there.

However, dividing taste and smell in this way is a very human-based way of looking at these types of sense organs. It applies to mammals and birds, but in many other groups of animals, there is little or no difference. For example, for a snail living in the water, "taste" and "smell" become almost the same.

UNLOCKING SMELLS
Biologists know little about the way that smells are converted from molecules floating in the air into nerve signals passing to the brain. The chief theory is that there is some form of "lock-and-key" mechanism. The sensory hairs that line the top of the nasal cavity, inside the nose, bear millions of nerve endings. In a human, there are about 15 million receptor cells in the nose, covering an area of about 1sq in. This is much less than in many mammals. A cat's smell receptors cover some 2½sq in, and a dog has a sensitive lining of 15sq in.

The receptors may have molecule-sized locks on their surface. Their keys are smell molecules. As a smell molecule reaches the nose it becomes trapped by the mucus overlying the sensory hairs, and passes through to slot into one of the locks. Fitting the key into the lock sparks off a nerve signal in some way. The key may be a chemical reaction between the smell molecule and the nerve ending; it could be the radiation which some

▼Most people recognize these seven distinct smells. We can probably call up memories in our mind's eye – or rather, our "mind's nose" – of what they smell like. The human nose can tell apart hundreds of different odors. Yet it is insensitive compared to many animals.

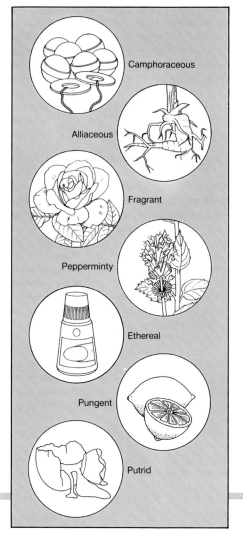

Camphoraceous

Alliaceous

Fragrant

Pepperminty

Ethereal

Pungent

Putrid

▼Taste buds in different parts of the tongue (1) respond most to one of the four main flavors that make up different tastes. A cutaway of the tongue (2) shows its surface, or epithelium, and the taste buds in deep grooves. Fluids collect in the grooves for tasting. There are also taste buds on the roof of the mouth, the throat and the tonsils. An enlargement of a single taste bud (3), with some 20 to 50 sensory and supporting cells grouped like segments of an orange.

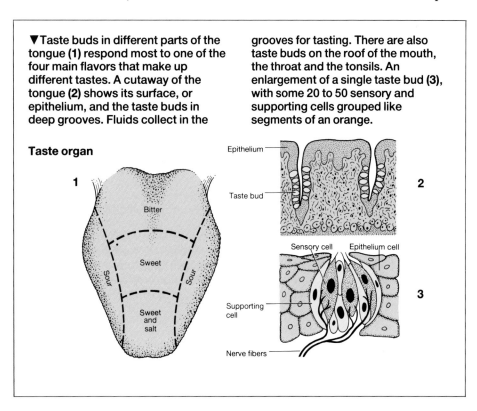

Taste organ

1
Bitter
Sour
Sweet
Sour
Sweet and salt

2
Epithelium
Taste bud

3
Sensory cell
Epithelium cell
Supporting cell
Nerve fibers

▼Many male moths have feathery antennae specialized for detecting a few odors which are important to the animal. This male Atlas moth has up to 10,000 receptors on his antennae, tuned to the female's sex-scent.

▲The snake's tongue "tastes" the air. As it flicks out, it picks up chemical signals. Back in the mouth, it is pushed into two pockets in the roof of the mouth, Jacobson's organs, where the chemicals are sensed.

▲A Brown hyena smothers grass with smelly substances from scent glands under its tail. The smell informs other hyenas that it has passed this way. Hyenas from other groups then know that the area is already occupied.

molecules give off; or it might be the particular properties of vibration that the molecule possesses.

THE "ODOR IMAGE"
Whatever the process, a complex pattern of nerve messages is sent to the brain from the smell receptors. How the brain interprets these messages is also not clear. Tests on mammalian smell receptors show that they are not very specific, but that each is sensitive to a variety of odors, and sends a varied set of signals to the smell centers in the brain.

It may be that the brain constructs a sort of "odor image" from the overall pattern of signals it receives, and does not rely on specific kinds of smell receptors for a particular sensation.

SMELLS TO ACT ON
Smells have a number of uses. In many creatures, they are used to find food. A

Polar bear can scent a seal carcass from 12mi. Deer are alerted by the merest whiff of a wolf on the breeze.

Smell also warns if food has gone bad or if it contains possibly harmful substances. Dogs, whose smelling abilities are up to 1,000 times better than ours, sniff any unfamiliar food cautiously before they take a bite.

Many animals use special smells called pheromones for communication. In moths, the female moth releases a type of odor known as a sex pheromone into the air from her body. This can be detected by male moths hundreds of yards away, using their feathery antennae. The male moth then follows the odor trail to find and mate with the female.

THE ONE-SCENT SENSE
One of these pheromones is bombykol. It is made by unmated female Silk moths, in glands on the abdomen.

This chemical has been produced in the laboratory, and tried on the male moths. Tests show that the male's antennae bear 17,000 smell receptors, and at least 300 of these must be stimulated before the moth takes any notice of the chemical.

Chemicals very similar to bombykol have also been made in the laboratory, in which just one atom of the bombykol molecule has been altered. The male moth is up to 1,000 times less sensitive to the smell of this altered molecule. So, although the male Silk moth is incredibly sensitive to the odor of real bombykol, it is likely that he can smell little else.

THE SMELL OF DANGER

Ants also use pheromones, of several different types. Scout ants lay a trail of odor when they find food, so that the other workers can follow this and bring the food back to the nest.

There are also alarm pheromones that warn the ant colony of danger, such as attack by an anteater. Upon smelling this warning signal in the air, the worker ants cluster round and try to defend the colony or repair the damage to the nest. Bees also use alarm pheromones to summon reinforcements. When a bee stings an intruder, she releases the pheromone and fellow workers come to help.

SMELL OR TASTE?

In insects, there are chemical receptors on the hairs of the body and limbs. It is often unclear whether, in human terms, these animals "taste" or "smell" a particular chemical. A fly has taste hairs on its feet and mouthparts.

◄A goosefish stalks a crab. Many crabs feed on carrion and are able to home in on dead creatures by using their sense of smell. The antennules carry delicate hair-like sense organs which respond to chemicals in the water. But these organs do not seem to have alerted the crab to the approaching fish.

This is a sensible design, since these are the first and second parts to come into contact with food.

In water-dwelling animals, all chemicals are water-borne. The distinction between smell and taste is even less clear. Fish have nostrils, and also taste buds in parts of their mouths and elsewhere. Catfish have so many taste receptors all over their bodies that they have sometimes been called swimming tongues.

Like moths in the insect group, some fish are extremely sensitive to specific smells. Salmon can find their way back over hundreds of miles to their home stream to spawn, partly by following its smell.

A QUESTION OF TASTE

It is generally recognized that there are four different kinds of tastes: sweet, acid (sour), salty and bitter. Each part of the human tongue responds best to one of these main flavors. The several tastes that we sense in our various foods, whether ordinary or exotic, are built up from mixtures of the four basic flavors plus odors. So food does not taste the same when we have a cold.

Before we can taste anything, it must be dissolved in saliva. It then spreads to touch taste buds, microscopic groups of cells in grooves and pits on the tongue. The cells have projections or taste hairs, yet another example of the sensory hair cell common in other senses. As with smell, the way that the dissolved chemicals make the cells fire off nerve signals is not clearly understood.

An adult has about 9,000 taste buds on the tongue. Babies and children have more, which die as they grow older. Like eyesight and hearing, taste becomes less sensitive with age. This may be why our tastes in food change and why some parents do not always agree with their children about horrible-tasting food or the foul-flavored medicines!

MUSCLES, SKELETONS

A large crab crawls hungrily over the sea bed. It notices a meaty-looking scallop, whose shell halves are slightly agape to reveal about 100 tiny blue eyes between them. As the crab nears, the scallop rapidly snaps its shell halves closed. Water shoots from between them, jerking the scallop backwards. It repeats the movement and rapidly "flaps" away from the startled crab.

The ability to move from place to place is known as locomotion. It has many different uses for an animal, including finding food and shelter, escaping from predators and locating a mate. Another type of movement happens inside the body. It moves body contents from one part to another, like food through the intestines or blood through the vessels.

Apart from the simplest creatures such as an amoeba, animal movement depends on muscles. Muscles are controlled by nerve signals, usually from the brain. However, muscles often act on the skeleton, which is the rigid structural framework of an animal. The muscle is attached to the skeleton via its long, tapering, rope-like end, called a tendon.

STRIPED OR SMOOTH?
There are two main types of muscle: smooth and striated. They are named from their appearance under the light microscope, striated muscle having regular light and dark stripes across its length. Striated muscles make those movements seen from outside, such as moving a limb or the whole body. An animal can make this kind of muscle move at will.

Smooth muscles lack stripes. They are concerned with the movements of internal organs. The control of these is largely automatic. For example, we do not control, or even usually notice, the movements of our intestines.

FIBERS AND FILAMENTS
A muscle is made of hundreds of small fibers lying side by side along its length. Inside each fiber are two kinds of even smaller filaments, thick and thin, arranged in regular bundles. These are, in fact, large molecules: the thick ones are a protein called myosin, and the thin ones are those of a protein called actin. The two sets of

▶Some birds must run before they can fly, to pick up speed for take-off. These Greater flamingos patter rapidly across the water while flapping their great wings, before becoming airborne.

▼One wingbeat of a duck in flight. The downstroke (the five stages below), with feathers spread, produces the lift that keeps the duck up. It also gives thrust to propel the bird forwards. On the upstroke (the five stages on the opposite page), the feathers are opened to let air through and the wing is tilted in line with the direction of flight, so giving the least air resistance.

filaments are linked by chemical bonds called cross-bridges. In relaxed muscle, these sets of filaments only just interlock with each other, like the fingertips of each hand held just touching. When the muscle is sent a signal by a nerve to become shorter, the two sets of filaments slide past each other, like the fingers of both hands moving together to interlock. The cross-bridges break and then reform with the next link along. As the filaments slide, the muscle shortens.

The strongest muscle, for its size, is that which keeps the two halves of a mussel shell closed. Among the fastest-acting muscles are the finger muscles of mice, which contract 15 times more quickly than the muscles in the leg of a tortoise.

SKELETONS INSIDE
There are numerous types of skeleton among animals. In the vertebrates the skeleton is made of bones and it is inside the body. Some bones are fixed firmly to each other, as with the parts of the skull. Others are linked by movable joints. The joints are lined with smooth, shiny cartilage, to help easy movement. Bone tissue is about two-thirds calcium phosphate crystals embedded in the type of fibrous protein known as collagen.

OUTER FRAME
Other animals have their body frameworks outside. Crabs and other crustaceans are encased in a hard outer shell, which becomes thinner at the joints to allow movement. The shell is up to about 90 percent calcium carbonate (the same chemical as chalk), with protein and another fibrous substance, chitin.

Many molluscs, including snails and scallops, have hard outer shells for skeletons. These are almost entirely

▲Airborne animals The Sugar glider (*Petaurus breviceps*) (1) glides on furred membranes. The Poplar admiral (*Limenitis populi*) (2) usually flaps but may glide on migration. The prehistoric pterosaur (*Pteranodon*) (3) was probably good at soaring. The Large mouse-eared bat (*Myotis myotis*) (4) is a true flier, unlike the gliding "Flying dragon" (*Draco spilopterus*) (5).

calcium carbonate, with less than 5 percent protein in the structure.

Insects also have a body with a hard outer casing, the cuticle. It is made up of chitin and various proteins.

Worms and similar creatures do not have hard, stiff parts in their bodies. Their "skeleton" comes from fluid under pressure, like water forced into a balloon. This is called a hydrostatic skeleton, and it is strong enough to enable an earthworm to tunnel through hard soil.

PULLING AGAINST PARTNERS

Muscles can only contract. They cannot actively lengthen. So how can animals carry out such complicated movements? The answer is that the muscles usually come in pairs. Each

◀Sharks lack swimbladders and so are not buoyant like other fish. They tend to sink unless they keep swimming. As they move forwards they obtain lift from the nose, wing-like fins and tail. This is a White-tipped reef shark.

63

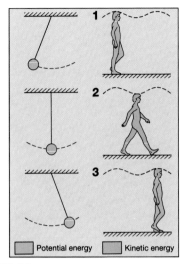

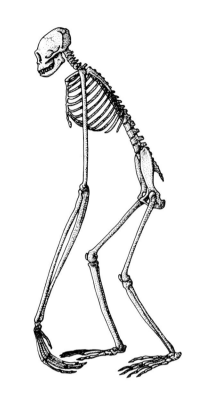

Walking

▲ A walking human is rather like a swinging pendulum. The pendulum and body are both at their highest points **(1)**. They use the pull of gravity to swing downwards and along **(2)**, and then, with only a little added effort, back up again **(3)**.

▼ The skeleton of a guenon, a type of monkey. Its limbs are all of roughly equal length, since this creature walks on all fours as it runs along branches and leaps through the trees of the African forests. Its long tail aids balancing and is used as a rudder when jumping through the air.

▲ In contrast to the guenon, the skeleton of this ape, an orang-utan, has quite different proportions. Its arms are extremely long because orangs move mainly by arm-swinging through the branches. Because they move this way apes do not need tails for balance.

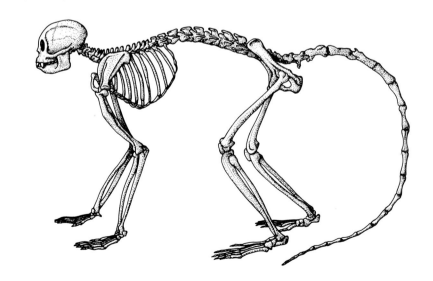

muscle in the pair reverses the effect of the other. As one contracts, it lengthens the other. We can see this in our own arm. Contract the muscle on the upper side of the upper arm, the biceps, and the elbow bends. Contract the muscle on the lower side, the triceps, and it straightens.

The same principle is used by worms. One set of muscles runs hoop-like around the worm's body, and another set runs lengthways along it. If the circular muscles contract, they make the whole body long and thin. Contraction of the muscles running lengthways makes it shorter and fatter.

PROPELLERS AND OARS

Water is a much thicker, denser substance than air. To move rapidly through it, an animal must be the right shape. This is the reason why most fast-swimming creatures, such as squid, dolphins, seals and speedy fish are long, slim and cigar-shaped.

There are four main kinds of swimming motion. One is rowing with oars. A water beetle has legs fringed with bristles. It pushes the legs back with the bristles spread out, and then brings them forwards with the bristles folded to reduce water resistance. In this manner it paddles along. Many slower-moving fish row with fins.

The penguin, and other birds that swim using their wings, move their wings up and down rather than forwards and backwards. The angle of the wing is adjusted to give it lift and push it forwards. A penguin really "flies" through the water.

Other water-dwellers swim by bending the body. S-shaped waves pass along the body as the muscles contract one after the other. Water snakes, leeches and fish such as eels use this method. In fish with powerful tails, like marlin and tuna, the tail is thrashed to and fro by the S-shaped curves, to give massive amounts of forward thrust. The fourth technique is the water-jet propulsion of squid

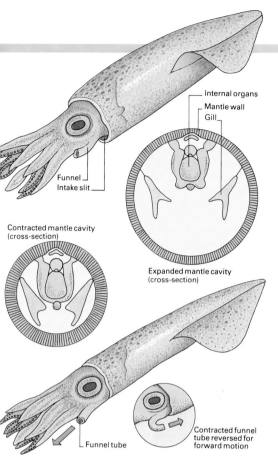

Internal organs
Mantle wall
Gill
Funnel
Intake slit

Contracted mantle cavity
(cross-section)

Expanded mantle cavity
(cross-section)

Funnel tube

Contracted funnel
tube reversed for
forward motion

▲Jet propulsion in the squid. Water is sucked into the main mantle cavity through a wide slit behind the eye (upper diagrams). Muscles in the mantle wall then contract to squeeze the water out of the thin funnel (lower diagrams). It spurts forwards in a powerful jet, pushing the squid backwards. The whole process is repeated rhythmically for smooth swimming.

and scallops. It gives great acceleration for escaping enemies.

TAKING TO THE AIR

Insects, birds and bats are the only true flying animals, able to make long and controlled flights using flapping wings. In the hovering flight of hummingbirds, and insects such as moths and hoverflies, the animal's body is more or less stationary and the wings move very quickly. In the forward flight of larger insects, bats and most birds, the body travels along and in many cases the wing acts like the aerofoil of an airplane wing, to give added lift.

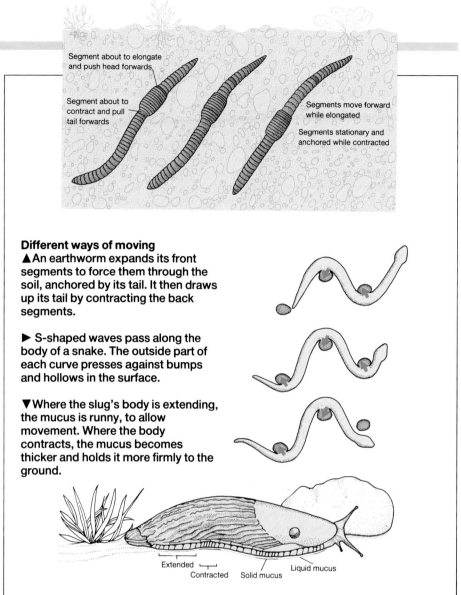

Segment about to elongate
and push head forwards

Segment about to
contract and pull
tail forwards

Segments move forward
while elongated

Segments stationary and
anchored while contracted

Different ways of moving
▲An earthworm expands its front segments to force them through the soil, anchored by its tail. It then draws up its tail by contracting the back segments.

► S-shaped waves pass along the body of a snake. The outside part of each curve presses against bumps and hollows in the surface.

▼Where the slug's body is extending, the mucus is runny, to allow movement. Where the body contracts, the mucus becomes thicker and holds it more firmly to the ground.

Extended
Contracted   Solid mucus   Liquid mucus

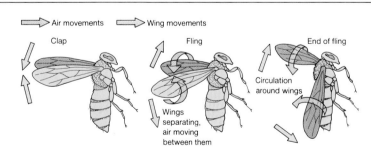

Air movements   Wing movements

Clap   Fling   End of fling

Circulation
around wings

Wings
separating,
air moving
between them

Clapping wings
▲Three stages in the "clap-and-fling" wingbeat method used by some hovering insects. The basic movements of the wing push air downwards to keep the insect airborne. In addition, the wings clap together over the back, and then fling outwards. The sudden rush of air into the space between the separating wings provides extra lift. In a mosquito, each wingbeat lasts only two-thousandths of a second.

BRAINS, NERVES

A soccer player receives a high pass on his chest and traps the ball with his foot. He dribbles past one opponent, and dodges around another. He approaches the goal and after a final sideways swerve, he kicks the ball hard towards the net – and scores! His brain has made dozens of muscles cooperate so that he can carry out the complicated actions of controlling the ball.

Animals use their muscles to make enormously powerful movements. Yet they can also make incredibly fine or gentle movements. But what makes the muscles do what they do? Why do they work together, rather than against one another?

THE NEED FOR NERVES

Control of the muscles is carried out by a system of nerves. The nerves in an animal's body work in a similar way to a telephone system. The "wires" of the system are the nerves themselves. They carry nerve messages, in the form of tiny electrical signals, quickly from one part of the body to another. This means body parts can keep in contact, so that one is affected by what happens in another.

In many animals there are "telephone exchanges" where messages are received, sorted and passed on to other body parts. These exchanges are made of many nerves gathered together. Such a bunch of nerves is called a ganglion. If there is a really large gathering of nerves, usually at the front of the animal, we call it a brain.

Some nerves send messages to muscles. Others carry messages into the body from sense organs such as eyes or touch receptors.

MESSAGE CARRIERS

The main part of a nerve is the nerve cell, or neuron. In most animals,

nerve cells have the same basic build. There is a cell body that contains the nucleus, and a long, thin extension like a wire, known as the axon. The axon acts like a wire, too, carrying signals along its length. At its tip, the axon splits into branches. Each branch ends in a button-shaped pad that almost touches the next cell, which may be another nerve cell or a muscle cell. At the other end of the nerve cell, projecting from the cell body, there are also many branches, called dendrites, that receive messages from other nerves (see page 70). The axons of some nerve cells are more than 3ft long, a great length for something so thin that it can only be seen under a microscope.

The thicker the axon of the nerve cell, the faster messages travel along it. In many animals, special thick axons carry messages that may mean life or death, making the animal take evasive action. For example, in the squid, giant axons run from the brain to the muscles that shoot water from its body, when the animal needs jet propulsion to escape from enemies. These axons are $\frac{1}{50}$in thick, which is huge for a cell! Because they are so large, they have been used by many scientists studying how nerves work.

Some kinds of nerve cell have a coating or sheath along much of the axon. This is made of myelin, a fatty substance. The myelin makes nerves work faster and more efficiently.

ONE-WAY TRAFFIC

When a message passes along a nerve cell, it is in the form of a small pulse of electricity. The fatty myelin sheath is an insulator, which is why it helps

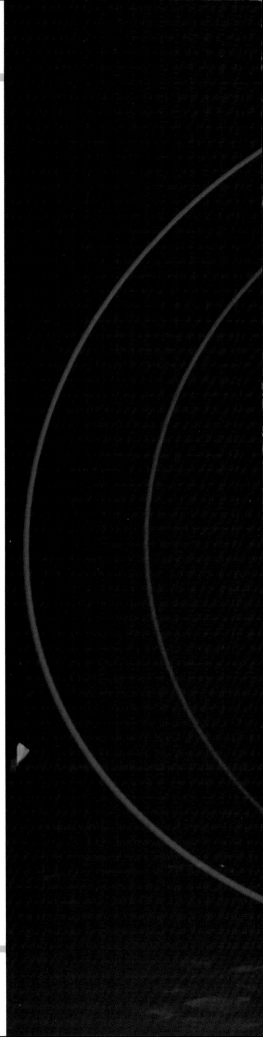

▶ British golfer Tony Jacklin prepares to strike the ball. The white line is the path taken by his right hand on a practice swing, and the red line traces the path of the golf club head. Actions such as this are the result of marvelous coordination of the senses and muscles, by the brain and nerves.

transmission. In theory, a pulse could travel either way along an axon. In fact, nerve signals only travel in one direction. This is because of the way that messages are passed to the next cell in the network.

There is a tiny gap (the synapse) between the "button" at the end of the axon, and the dendrite of the next nerve cell. When a signal reaches the button it produces a chemical that travels across the gap. This makes a change in the cell membrane of the next cell, which starts a new electrical pulse traveling through that cell. Only buttons at the end of the axon produce the chemical, and not the dendrites of the next cell. So the nerve signal can only travel one way.

ALL OR NOTHING

A single nerve cell cannot transmit different strengths of signal. Either it is inactive, with no pulses at all, or a standard strength pulse travels along it. The only way it can change its signal is by sending pulses at a faster or slower rate.

Other ways in which different messages can be sent between parts of the body include using more or fewer nerve cells, or by using different combinations of nerve cells.

WIRE NETTING

Some of the simpler multi-celled animals, such as jellyfish and sea anemones, have their nerve cells connected in a network around the body, which looks like wire netting or a fishing net. For simple swimming, a nerve signal can spread around the net and start the muscles contracting in the correct order.

For a circular animal, the system seems fine. When a sea anemone is touched, a signal goes through the nerve net to contract the stalk muscles as an escape reaction. It is less easy to see how such a nervous system can control a sea anemone's movements as it "shuffles" from a rock on to a shell

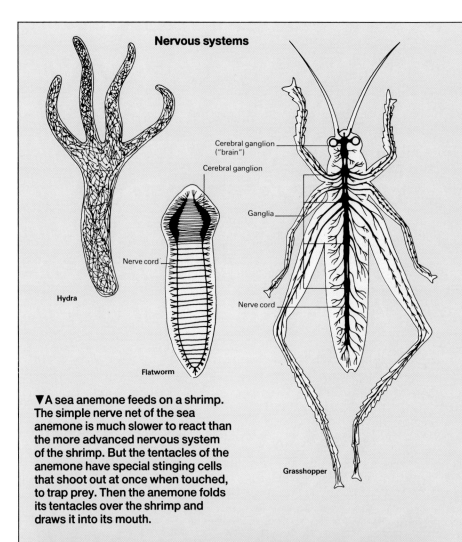

Nervous systems

Hydra

Flatworm

Cerebral ganglion ("brain")

Cerebral ganglion

Ganglia

Nerve cord

Nerve cord

Grasshopper

▼A sea anemone feeds on a shrimp. The simple nerve net of the sea anemone is much slower to react than the more advanced nervous system of the shrimp. But the tentacles of the anemone have special stinging cells that shoot out at once when touched, to trap prey. Then the anemone folds its tentacles over the shrimp and draws it into its mouth.

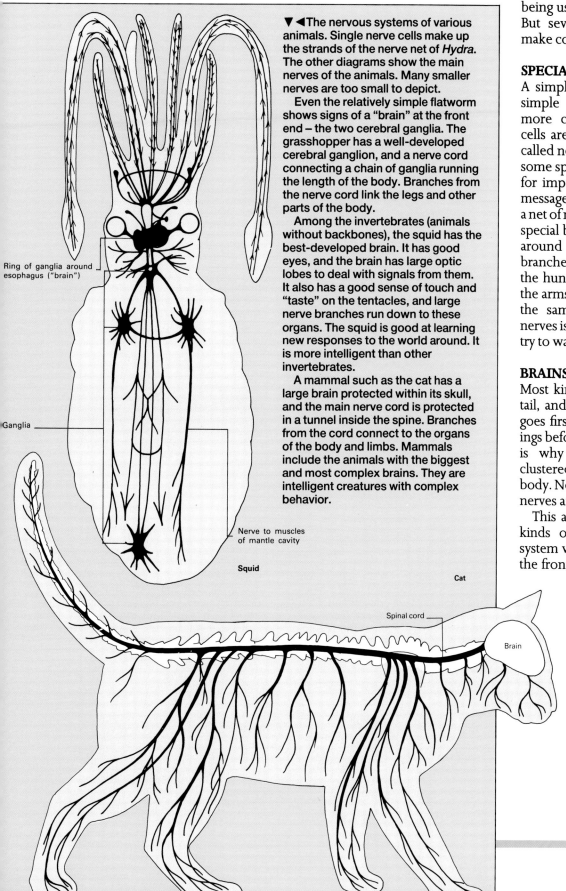

▼◄The nervous systems of various animals. Single nerve cells make up the strands of the nerve net of *Hydra*. The other diagrams show the main nerves of the animals. Many smaller nerves are too small to depict.

Even the relatively simple flatworm shows signs of a "brain" at the front end – the two cerebral ganglia. The grasshopper has a well-developed cerebral ganglion, and a nerve cord connecting a chain of ganglia running the length of the body. Branches from the nerve cord link the legs and other parts of the body.

Among the invertebrates (animals without backbones), the squid has the best-developed brain. It has good eyes, and the brain has large optic lobes to deal with signals from them. It also has a good sense of touch and "taste" on the tentacles, and large nerve branches run down to these organs. The squid is good at learning new responses to the world around. It is more intelligent than other invertebrates.

A mammal such as the cat has a large brain protected within its skull, and the main nerve cord is protected in a tunnel inside the spine. Branches from the cord connect to the organs of the body and limbs. Mammals include the animals with the biggest and most complex brains. They are intelligent creatures with complex behavior.

Ring of ganglia around esophagus ("brain")

Ganglia

Nerve to muscles of mantle cavity

Squid

Cat

Spinal cord

Brain

being used as home by a hermit crab. But several kinds of anemone can make complex movements like this.

SPECIAL PATHS
A simple nerve net is enough for a simple animal. But to coordinate more complex animals, the nerve cells are bundled together as groups called nerves. These are laid out along some special pathways that are routes for important or commonly needed messages. A starfish, for example, has a net of nerves around the outside, but special bundles of nerves make a ring around the middle of the body, with branches into the arms. These control the hundreds of tiny tube feet under the arms, making sure they all walk in the same direction. If the ring of nerves is damaged, different arms may try to walk in different directions.

BRAINS AND CORDS
Most kinds of animal have a head, a tail, and two similar sides. The head goes first, so it meets new surroundings before the rest of the animal. This is why sense organs are usually clustered in the head at the front of the body. Nerves run from these, so many nerves are clustered at the head too.

This arrangement has led to many kinds of animal having a nervous system with a "brain" of some kind at the front. A large bundle of nerves (a nerve cord) projects from the back of the brain, into the body. In an animal such as the human, the brain and main nerve cord (spinal cord) is called the central nervous system. Branches from this link to all parts of the body.

A simple animal like a flatworm shows the beginnings of such a system. Worms and insects have more developed brains and nerve cords, although the details of the parts differ. In insects, for example, the main nerve cord runs along the underside, and not along the upper side. In other complex animals the shapes and sizes of nervous systems vary, but the basic organization is similar.

BRAIN SIZE
As a rough-and-ready rule, we might expect that the bigger the brain, the more intelligent the animal. This is not entirely true. An elephant has a bigger

Types of nerve cell

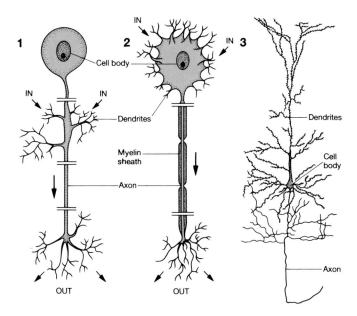

▲A Crayfish motor nerve cell (1), or neuron. (Motor nerves carry signals from the brain to muscles.) Other nerves connect with dendrites a little way down the axon. In a human motor neuron (2), the incoming connections are to dendrites on the cell body. Nerve signals pass on from the far end of the axon. In a brain neuron (3), the dendrites are finely branched.

Brains
▼▶The brains of vertebrates differ in overall size, and also in the relative sizes of their parts. In the lower vertebrates such as fish (1) and amphibians (2) the medulla, the part of the brain responsible for automatic control of simple body functions, is the largest part. In the more complex reptiles (3), birds (4) and mammals (5), including humans (6), other parts of the brain become more important. The cerebellum (blue) coordinates the balance and control of movements. The cerebrum (brown), originally a small area at the front of the brain, has expanded in the human to cover the rest of the brain. Its huge numbers of nerve cells allow our intelligent and varied behavior.

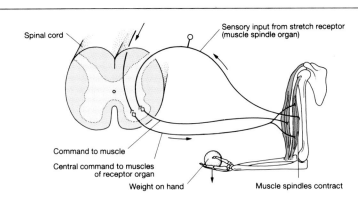

▲How a simple reflex works. Placing a weight in someone's hand causes the hand to move downwards. This stretches the muscle spindle organ and starts nerve signals. The signals travel to the spinal column, where the nerve's ending connects to a motor neuron running to the arm muscle. Signals pass along this and command the muscle to contract, moving the hand up to support the extra weight. The whole sequence is automatic.

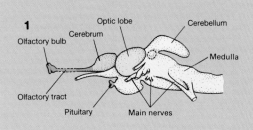

brain than a human. It is intelligent compared to many animals, but not compared to us. Big animals usually have large brains simply because so many nerves supply their big bodies.

A better guide to intelligence, though still not completely true, is brain size compared to body weight. Here, humans come out on top. There are also ways of packing in more nerve cells to increase "brain power." For example, the surface of the human brain is folded and crossed by many little valleys which increase its surface area, and which are lacking in less "brainy" animals.

A simple animal with a simple life-style may need few nerve cells. Some roundworms manage with less than 100 in their body. In contrast an active, alert, intelligent animal may have millions. An octopus has up to 200 million nerve cells in its brain

alone. A human brain contains 10 billion (10,000,000,000) nerve cells.

BRAINS IN ACTION

How does a brain work? We know part of the story, but not all of the details. It is known for some animals that nerve cells with a particular function always occur in the same place. For example, in a crab, two nerve cells are responsible for making the eye "blink" into its socket. They are the same shape and in the same place in every member of the species. The locations of cells involved in other simple actions are also known. But when it comes to looking at a whole brain, the sheer scale and complexity of its construction makes it hard to study.

A single nerve cell in a human brain may have more than 250,000 connections from other nerve cells joining to

it. In every cubic inch of the outer layer of the brain, there may be over 10,000mi of tiny fibers connecting the cells. We can recognize some of the main pathways in the brain, but we rarely know exactly which cell is connected to which.

In spite of this, scientists have shown that some parts of the brain have particular jobs. In an octopus brain, one area seems to be responsible for learning. If this part is destroyed, the octopus can no longer learn, although in other respects it works well enough. In humans, different areas of the brain receive input from different parts of the body. Similarly, there are specific areas responsible for moving the muscles of particular limbs. Such aspects of the mind as memory, emotions, learning, dreams and language ability also seem linked to a particular part of the brain.

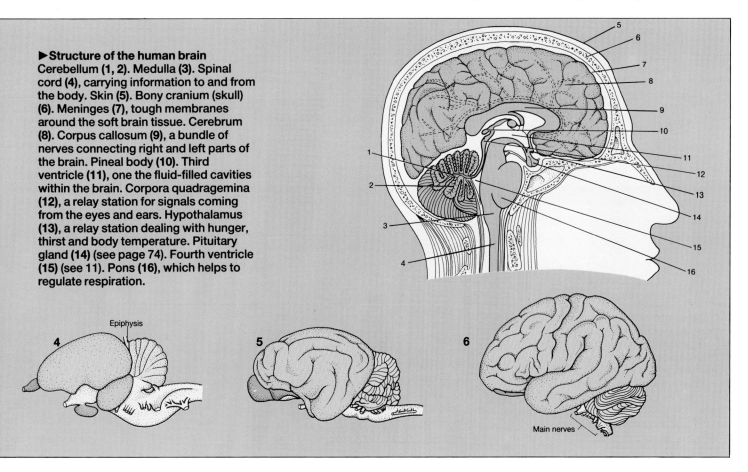

▶**Structure of the human brain**
Cerebellum (1, 2). Medulla (3). Spinal cord (4), carrying information to and from the body. Skin (5). Bony cranium (skull) (6). Meninges (7), tough membranes around the soft brain tissue. Cerebrum (8). Corpus callosum (9), a bundle of nerves connecting right and left parts of the brain. Pineal body (10). Third ventricle (11), one the fluid-filled cavities within the brain. Corpora quadragemina (12), a relay station for signals coming from the eyes and ears. Hypothalamus (13), a relay station dealing with hunger, thirst and body temperature. Pituitary gland (14) (see page 74). Fourth ventricle (15) (see 11). Pons (16), which helps to regulate respiration.

Epiphysis

4   5   6

Main nerves

HORMONES

Walking down a jungle path, a villager suddenly finds his path blocked by a leopard. Almost immediately, his heart starts pumping harder and faster. His hair stands on end and the pupils of his eyes widen. Both he and the cat are frightened, yet alert and ready to run. The leopard moves off at last. Safe again, the man's body gradually relaxes.

The "emergency reactions" that take place in a frightened person prepare the body for fleeing or fighting the danger. The airways widen and breathing increases, the surface blood vessels contract and make the skin pale, and more blood is sent to the muscles. More sugar is released into the blood to provide easily used energy. The heart steps up its work. In ourselves, we notice other reactions, like the hair on the back of our necks standing up.

Similar reactions take place in other animals. A frightened cat's heart beats faster and its fur stands on end.

These "fight or flight" reactions are caused by a chemical, adrenaline, flooding through the body. It is made in special glands, the adrenals, and is released into the bloodstream in times of stress. The chemical travels rapidly around the body in the blood and affects just a few "target organs," such as the heart and lungs, in the ways described.

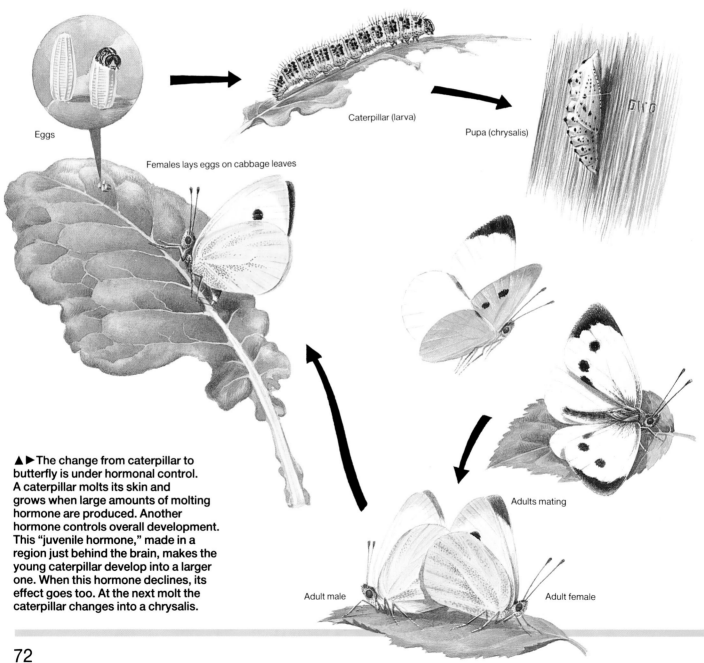

Eggs

Females lays eggs on cabbage leaves

Caterpillar (larva)

Pupa (chrysalis)

Adults mating

Adult male

Adult female

▲▶ The change from caterpillar to butterfly is under hormonal control. A caterpillar molts its skin and grows when large amounts of molting hormone are produced. Another hormone controls overall development. This "juvenile hormone," made in a region just behind the brain, makes the young caterpillar develop into a larger one. When this hormone declines, its effect goes too. At the next molt the caterpillar changes into a chrysalis.

LONG-LASTING MESSAGE

The chemical adrenaline acts as a messenger. Such a chemical, creating an effect in another part of the body from where it was produced, is called a hormone. Many hormones act in our bodies, and in those of other animals. Like nerves, hormones allow body parts to communicate with each other. But although a few produce effects very fast, like adrenaline, many hormones have a longer-term action. Their effects happen over days or months, rather than in a flash, like a nerve's action.

Hormones are powerful chemicals. They circulate in the body in very low amounts but have large effects. They are made in certain organs called endocrine glands. These glands have no special ducts or other outlets. They release their hormones into the surrounding fluids, to be carried away in the blood.

BEARDS AND ANTLERS

One of the first hormones to be discovered was the male sex hormone, called testosterone. This is made in the testes, the sex glands of male vertebrates. It causes growth and development of the male sex organs. It also triggers "secondary sexual characteristics," which include a deep voice, and facial hair in men. In deer, the male sex hormone causes larger body size than the female, and the development of antlers. In chickens, testosterone produces the rooster's fine tail feathers, large comb, and his ability to crow.

Hormones can affect behavior as well as bodies. Male hormones make animals such as stallions or bulls more

▶A newly-emerged adult of the Mexican grasshopper *Taeniopoda auricornis*. The molted skin of its previous stage is still attached to the plant. Molting hormone is made by a gland in the thorax, the central part of the body. This gland is itself controlled by a hormone made in the brain.

aggressive than the females. For thousands of years, farmers have known that castration (removal of the testes) quietens down such animals. A castrated ox, known as a bullock, is a placid animal. Only in the last hundred years have scientists discovered why this should be.

HORMONES AND CHANGE

Many hormones help to maintain the balance of chemicals in the body. But some bring change. The change from tadpole to frog is brought about when the tadpole's pituitary gland at the base of the brain is stimulated, perhaps by an increase in temperature. The pituitary releases a hormone which activates another gland, the thyroid, in the neck. This makes the hormone thyroxine.

Thyroxine affects some parts of the tadpole's body by making them grow fast, or change shape, and it causes the tail and gills to shrink. The result is a change from tadpole to frog. If, for some reason, no thyroxine is produced, then the tadpole stays as a tadpole. On the other hand, miniature frogs can be produced from young tadpoles by feeding them extra amounts of thyroxine. The axolotl, a Mexican salamander, normally keeps its gills and stays in water all its life. If it is fed extra thyroxine, it becomes a land salamander.

LIFE PUT ON HOLD

When days are short, in spring, the female silk moth *Bombyx mori* lays colorless eggs that soon hatch and develop. When the days are long, in summer, she lays colored eggs that have a long resting period. They do not hatch until early next spring. The difference is because of a hormone produced by the moth's brain, which is only made when there are long periods of daylight. The hormone affects the ovary, so that the special resting eggs develop.

FEEDBACK

The quantities of many hormones are controlled by "feedback." If enough hormone is circulating in the body, this slows down production by the gland. This is called negative feedback. It is typical for many of the glands that control the balance of chemicals in the body.

In a few cases, hormones produce positive feedback – they encourage the gland to produce even more of themselves. This happens when the amphibian thyroid gland secretes thyroxine. It may explain why, after weeks as a tadpole, the change to an adult comes with a rush.

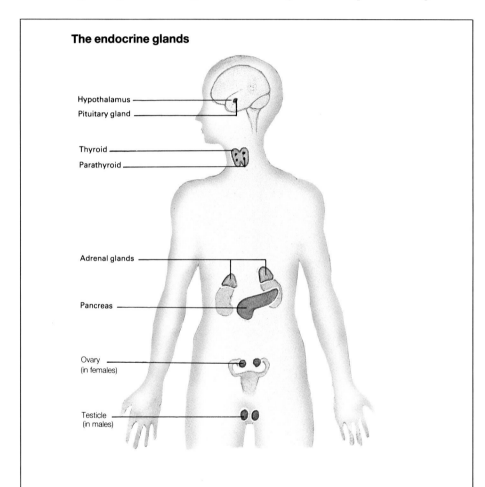

The endocrine glands

Hypothalamus
Pituitary gland

Thyroid
Parathyroid

Adrenal glands

Pancreas

Ovary
(in females)

Testicle
(in males)

The thyroid controls energy use in the body. With the parathyroids, it also affects calcium levels. The pancreas hormones control sugar balance. The adrenals above the kidneys make hormones that regulate salt balance in the body, plus some sex hormones. Also they produce adrenaline and other hormones which help the body react to emergencies. Testes (in males) or ovaries (in females) make hormones affecting reproduction and sexual development. Some of the pituitary's hormones control other endocrine glands. The hypothalamus links the brain to the pituitary.

▶Mating lions. Their behavior and appearance are influenced by hormones. The male hormones produced by the testes of the male lion make his body large and his mane grow. They also affect his voice, so that he has a deep-throated roar. Female hormones from the lioness's ovaries help bring her body into breeding condition, and influence her readiness to mate.

CELL DIVISION, GENETICS

A family lines up for a photograph. The oldest boy looks very like his father. His sister looks like her father too, with dark hair and dark eyes. But her younger sister and the baby brother take after their mother, with fair hair and small noses. The photographer notices and wonders why some children look like one parent, while others take after the other parent.

For thousands of years, people have realized that children tend to look like their parents. Young animals, too, usually take after their parents rather than other members of their species. What makes us look like our parents? Indeed, what makes dogs look like dogs, and not like giraffes or squirrels? Now we know that the answer lies in almost every cell of an animal's body.

MENDEL'S PEAS

The first experiments about family likeness, which eventually led to the answer, were made by a monk called Gregor Mendel in the mid-1800s. He worked with plants rather than animals. He grew certain types and colors of peas, then carefully bred the offspring together in various combinations. He made meticulous notes and counted the number of offspring with particular features, such as color, plant size, and wrinkliness.

When Mendel bred tall pea plants with short ones, all the offspring were tall. But if he bred some of these offspring together, one quarter of their offspring were short plants. His experiments seemed to show that one feature was passed on more strongly than another. It took over, or dominated, the weaker feature. But the characteristic that did not show in the offspring had not disappeared entirely. It re-emerged, in turn, in some of their offspring.

This experiment, as well as others Mendel made, could be explained if every plant had two sets of the characters. One was inherited from its father, and one from its mother. When it bred, each of the pair of characters was passed on separately, or independently. Nowadays, we call the characters that Gregor Mendel discovered "genes."

TALL AND SHORT

In the tall and short peas, for example, the pure-bred tall peas each had two genes for being tall. The pure-bred short peas each had two genes for being short. Together, they produced offspring which each had one gene for being tall, and one for being short. But the gene for being short was overshadowed by the tallness gene. In other words, the tallness gene was "dominant," and the gene for being short was "recessive." But when this generation bred together, some of the offspring (one in four) had both genes producing shortness, so these peas were short.

Since Mendel's time we have found that all living things work in much the same way as peas, passing on genes to their offspring. In some cases the genes behave in a more complicated way, but the basic principles are the same. Mendel, the discoverer of these principles, was unfortunate in that, during his lifetime, his experiments did not lead to a greater understanding of the science of genes. Today, we know this science as genetics and it is fast growing in importance and in its ability to produce practical results.

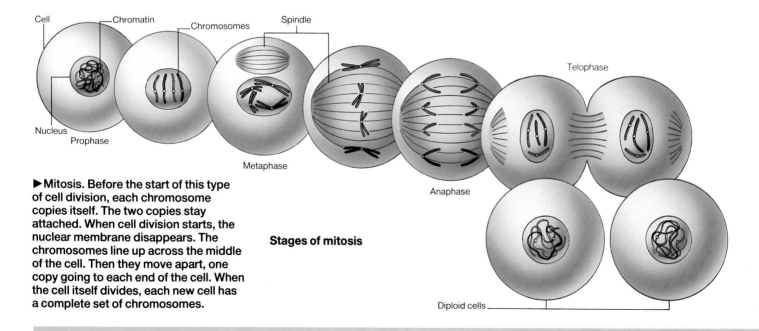

▶Mitosis. Before the start of this type of cell division, each chromosome copies itself. The two copies stay attached. When cell division starts, the nuclear membrane disappears. The chromosomes line up across the middle of the cell. Then they move apart, one copy going to each end of the cell. When the cell itself divides, each new cell has a complete set of chromosomes.

Stages of mitosis

20TH-CENTURY SCIENCE

From the early years of the 20th century, the science of genetics began to progress. Many new experiments were carried out, and Mendel's pioneering work was recognized. The basis for the way characters were inherited was discovered in cells. From the 1950s onwards, the search was on to discover the molecular basis of genetics. The second half of the 20th century has seen huge leaps in our understanding of genes and molecular biology.

VITAL CHROMOSOMES

Scientists realized that in each cell there are parts which are passed on in much the same way as genes. These parts are called chromosomes, and they are in the cell's nucleus. Much of the time they are difficult to see, but

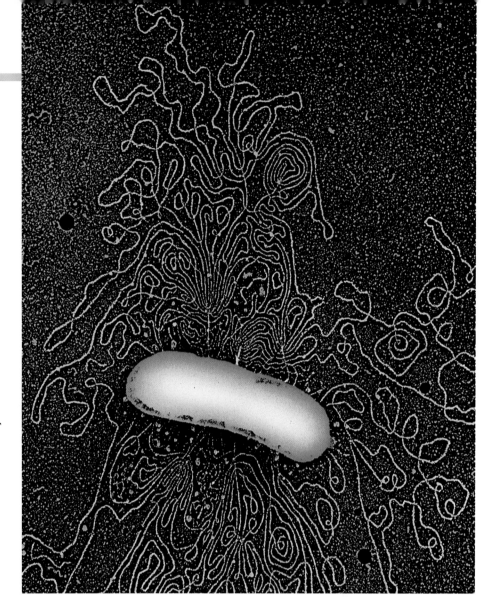

▶The chromosome of a bacterium. This *Escherischia coli* bacterium has been treated so that its cell wall has broken down and released the chromosome contents. The long strands seen all around it are normally folded inside the cell. They contain all the information required to make the substances that it needs during its life, and to pass on its "blueprint" to the next generation.

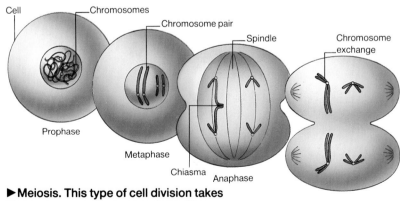

Cell — Chromosomes — Chromosome pair — Spindle — Chromosome exchange

Prophase

Metaphase

Chiasma   Anaphase

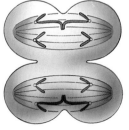

Telophase

Haploid cells

Stages of meiosis

▶Meiosis. This type of cell division takes place when sperms or eggs form. The chomosomes come together in matching pairs along the middle of the cell. One of each pair goes to each end as the cell divides. Then each chromosome splits in two, the two halves move apart, and the cell divides again. Each of the four new cells contains only half the original number.

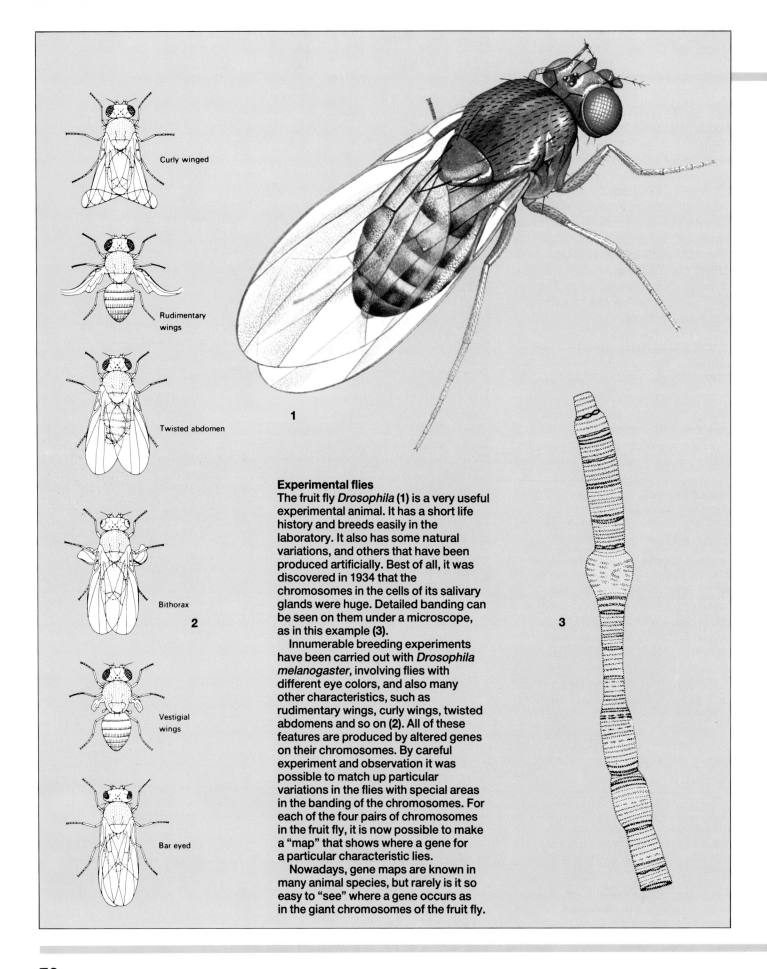

Curly winged

Rudimentary wings

Twisted abdomen

Bithorax

Vestigial wings

Bar eyed

1

2

3

Experimental flies

The fruit fly *Drosophila* (1) is a very useful experimental animal. It has a short life history and breeds easily in the laboratory. It also has some natural variations, and others that have been produced artificially. Best of all, it was discovered in 1934 that the chromosomes in the cells of its salivary glands were huge. Detailed banding can be seen on them under a microscope, as in this example (3).

Innumerable breeding experiments have been carried out with *Drosophila melanogaster*, involving flies with different eye colors, and also many other characteristics, such as rudimentary wings, curly wings, twisted abdomens and so on (2). All of these features are produced by altered genes on their chromosomes. By careful experiment and observation it was possible to match up particular variations in the flies with special areas in the banding of the chromosomes. For each of the four pairs of chromosomes in the fruit fly, it is now possible to make a "map" that shows where a gene for a particular characteristic lies.

Nowadays, gene maps are known in many animal species, but rarely is it so easy to "see" where a gene occurs as in the giant chromosomes of the fruit fly.

when a cell prepares to divide, they become more visible, and they can be stained with a special dye to make them easier to see when viewed under a microscope. (Chromosome means "colored body.")

Before a cell begins dividing, the chromosomes become rod-shaped. As it divides, the chromosomes are divided equally between the two new cells. But the way in which this happens differs according to whether it is a normal cell dividing to make two more normal body cells (the process called mitosis), or a cell dividing to make sperm or eggs (the process known as meiosis).

An ordinary body cell contains an even number of chromosomes which can be matched in pairs. Each member of a pair is the same size and shape, and controls the same characteristics, as its partner. This means it carries the same genes. So in a pea, the genes that decide whether the plant will be tall or short occur on paired chromosomes.

Before a body cell divides, it doubles up its chromosomes. When it divides, a complete set of all the pairs is passed to each of the new cells. But when sex cells form, the doubling does not happen. Division takes place so that only one chromosome from each pair goes into the resulting egg or sperm. So an egg cell or sperm cell has only half the number of chromosomes of a normal body cell. This "half set" of chromosomes is called the haploid number.

When a sperm fertilizes an egg, two half sets come together to make a full set. This full set is called the diploid number of chromosomes.

X AND Y
All the chromosomes in a diploid cell come in pairs. The two chromosomes in each pair look much the same – with one exception. In many animals, scientists have found that the partners in one pair of chromosomes do not look the same. One chromosome is larger than the other. This pair of chromosomes seems responsible for the difference between the sexes.

The larger of the chromosomes in an uneven pair is usually called an X chromosome and the smaller one a Y. In people and other mammals, an individual with two X chromosomes in the pair is female. An individual with one X and one Y is male. This is not always the case in other animals. Among birds, females have an XY pair and males have XX.

As well as having genes which control sex, the X and Y chromosomes have other genes that affect other body features. So sometimes we find features that are "sex-linked." These occur only, or much more commonly, in one sex rather than the other. In people, for example, color blindness is much more common in men than in women. In cats, ginger coloring nearly always means a male cat, while tortoiseshell coloring indicates a female.

WHAT'S IN A CHROMOSOME?
As we have seen with the X and Y chromosomes, each chromosome can carry more than one gene. In fact, scientists have been able to find dozens of genes on a single chromosome, and map their positions along it. But what are genes, and what is a chromosome made of? Chromosomes contain large amounts of a substance called deoxyribonucleic acid, or DNA for short. This is a very

►The first experiments in the science of genetics were begun in 1856 by Gregor Mendel, an Austrian monk. He carried out careful work breeding peas, and found that characteristics were always passed on in a certain way. His work was not really appreciated in his lifetime, but experiments like his became the basis of the modern science of genetics. He took great care in the way he designed and carried out his experiments. By counting and keeping records he was able to show the way in which living things passed on their characteristics.

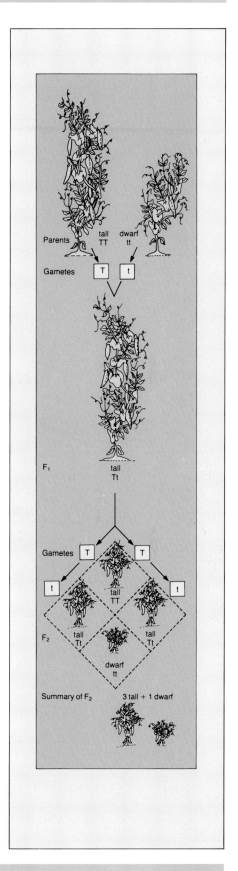

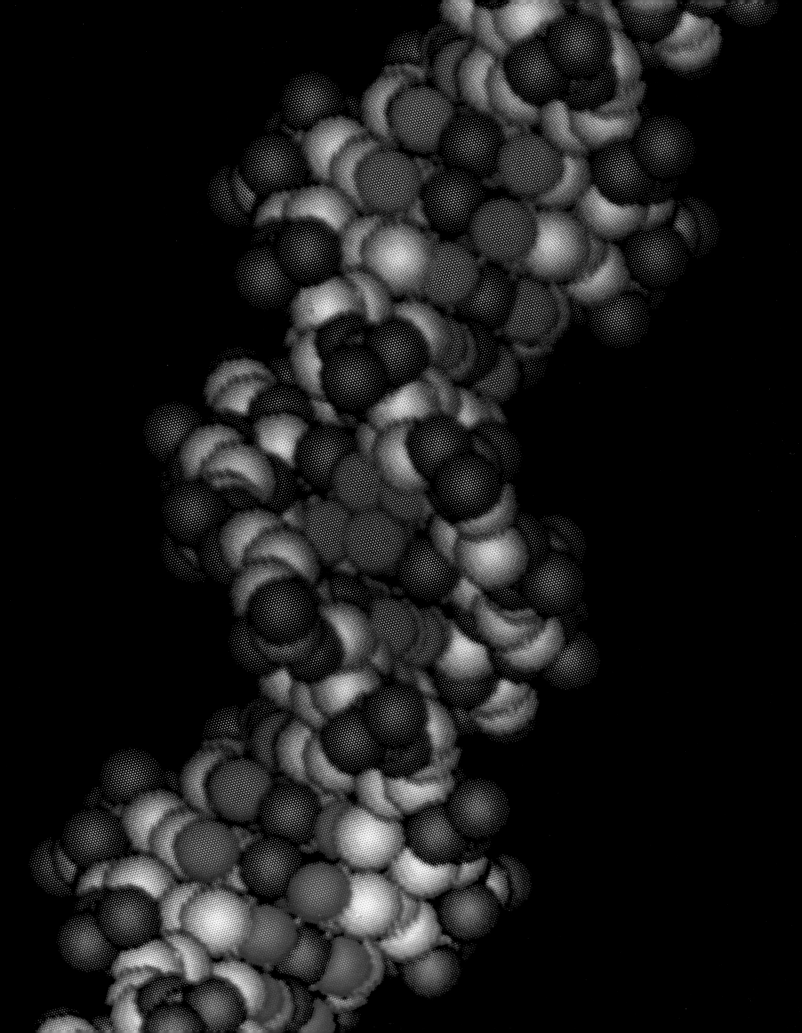

long molecule which is really a chain of repeating units. There may be tens of thousands of these units in a single DNA molecule. It is like a very long, thin thread, but in a dividing cell it coils up into the chromosomes we recognize. This long molecule carries a chemical code that holds all the basic instructions needed to make a working animal cell and, in the end, the whole animal.

THE STRUCTURE OF DNA
Although it is such a big molecule, DNA is built up in a fairly simple way.

◄A model shows that characteristic double helix structure of part of a DNA molecule. In every animal cell, DNA molecules carry the coded information needed for all its life processes.

It consists of two strands joined together. Each strand has a "back-bone" of molecules of a sugar, deoxyribose, connected to one another. The strand has a helical shape, rather like a coiled spring. The two strands are like two intertwined springs, held together by chemical attachments.

Each of the sugar molecules along the strand has attached to it a molecule of a substance known as a base. There are many kinds of base, but DNA has only four. They are called guanine, cytosine, adenine and thymine. One strand of the DNA is connected to the other by links between these bases, in the same way that rungs of a ladder connect the upright parts. The bases only fit together in two ways. Guanine links

with cytosine. Adenine links with thymine. So, if it is known which bases are attached to sugars along one strand of DNA, it is evident which bases will be attached with absolute certainty to the opposite strand.

This arrangement also gives the DNA molecule a perfect means of copying itself. If the two strands of DNA come apart, then new material can be assembled to make two new strands, which form double strands with those already there. The new double strands each have the same sequence of bases as the old. This is the secret of life – how DNA copies itself to make the next generation.

In the chromosomes of the cell's nucleus, then, are DNA molecules that can copy themselves. The DNA

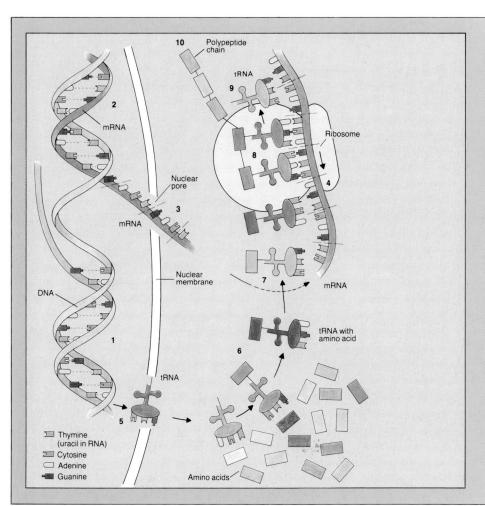

10 Polypeptide chain
tRNA
9
2
mRNA
Ribosome
8
Nuclear pore
3
mRNA
4
Nuclear membrane
7
mRNA
DNA
tRNA with amino acid
1
6
tRNA
5
Amino acids

Thymine (uracil in RNA)
Cytosine
Adenine
Guanine

Making a protein
◄The "factories" of the body cells are the small structures called ribosomes (4), which are in the cytoplasm of the cell. The instructions for what is to be made come from the nucleus. Part of the DNA in there unwinds (2) and a chain of messenger RNA (mRNA) forms. The sequence of bases on this (shown as green, blue, yellow or brown attachments) is determined by the bases opposite them on the DNA strand. The messenger RNA moves into the cytoplasm through gaps in the nuclear membrane (3).

Another type of RNA, transfer RNA (shown as tRNA in the diagram), picks up particular amino acids (6) in the cytoplasm. (Amino acids are shown as colored rectangles.) In the ribosome the transfer RNA links temporarily to a particular site on the messenger RNA, into which its bases fit (7). This gives a chance for the amino acid it is carrying to join the next amino acid along, to form a chain (8). The transfer RNA comes unstuck from both the amino acid it was carrying and the messenger RNA, and floats off into the cytoplasm (9). A chain of amino acids (a polypeptide chain) is created (10), and this forms the basis of a protein.

It takes only one second to form a chain of 4,000 amino acids.

"formula" of an animal (or a plant) is passed to every cell of the body as the cells form by cell division. The formula is also passed on to each of the eggs and sperm.

BUILDING BODIES
But how does the DNA molecule tell a cell what to be, and what to make? The sequence of bases along a DNA strand works like a kind of code.

The structure of a cell and its workings are brought about largely by protein molecules. A code which specifies which proteins are made is therefore a code which specifies a particular kind of cell or animal. The code which is built into the structure of DNA can do this.

A section of three bases in DNA makes the "code name" for one of about twenty kinds of amino acid. These acids are the building blocks which make proteins. A line of thousands of bases along a DNA molecule can code for whole strings of different amino acids. These amino acids, brought together in the correct order, form a protein molecule.

This "manufacture" does not take place in the nucleus itself. The DNA is like a "blueprint," which sends its instructions to the "factory" in the cytoplasm of the cell (see page 81).

WHEN COPYING GOES WRONG
DNA is a very long molecule. It carries an enormous amount of information in its codes. It has a mechanism for exactly copying itself. But, like any procedure where huge numbers of steps are involved, occasional mistakes occur.

In DNA, a base may get lost or added in copying. A tiny part of the molecule may become broken off. The result may be a copy that is not exact. Some of these copies will not work. If they are present in eggs and sperm they may be infertile, or the resulting embryo cannot develop properly or survive.

But some of these "different" copies may still result in a slightly different animal that works perfectly well. It is different, but not in dangerous ways.

Occasionally a new variation on DNA may actually be better than the original. This is probably how new animals have taken over from ancestors in the course of evolution.

VARIATION ON A THEME
The study of DNA has shown that this enormously long molecule has the capacity to code for huge numbers of substances. In a chromosome, some of the DNA is probably redundant, in that it repeats another section. Or it produces no effect at all.

Scientists have also realized that much of DNA, far from dealing with "life and death" necessities, can vary quite a bit, producing small and fairly random variations on a theme. Many groups of animals in nature seem to have quite a lot of natural variation in their genes. In some cases this is linked to their survival. For example, some snail species come in several color varieties, and each variety survives best in different conditions. But

▼ Genetic variation in the European adder. Brown or silver colors are found, with the typical zigzag marks along the back. Very dark individuals are also seen. Many are females. Many silvery snakes are males.

in many cases the variations seem to be neither good nor bad. Consider humans, who may be tall or short, fat or thin, and have a variety of hair, eye and skin colors. Their genes are all slightly different, but it makes little difference to their survival.

MULES: THE END OF THE LINE
In most cases the difference between species of animals, in their structure and behavior, is so great that they do not try to breed with one another. Even if they did, they would normally find that their combined chromosomes and DNA would not provide a working blueprint for an animal.

But there are a few exceptions. Some species are so closely related, with similar chromosomes and DNA, that they can produce offspring. Some kinds of pheasant, for example, can breed together to produce hybrids.

▼All of these colors can be seen in shells of one group of the Banded snail *Cepaea nemoralis*. In open areas pale shells are often common. In woods a high proportion have dark shells. Poorly camouflaged snails are probably soon caught by predators and never breed.

▲A zebroid. A cross between horse and zebra, two species similar enough to interbreed and produce offspring. But the chromosomes from the mother and father are not alike enough to make satisfactory eggs or sperm, so the zebroid cannot breed.

Lions and tigers living in captivity sometimes produce young. A male donkey may breed with a female horse, who gives birth to a mule.

In some cases the young produced by these mixtures are actually bigger or stronger than their parents. Mules are known for their toughness. But they are the end of the line. In nearly every case, these mixed-species hybrids cannot themselves breed and produce offspring. Almost certainly this is because of the mechanics of cell division. Their chromosomes are not true pairs, and so they cannot divide properly to form eggs or sperm.

REPRODUCTION, GROWTH

A young Blue tit's head peeps out from a hole in a tree. Then its owner appears, and launches into the air. It is followed by another, and still more, 13 in all. A pair of Blue tits have reared their young, who are now leaving the nest.

▼Cell divisions in the testes (shown blue) and in the ovary (shown pink). In many animals these sex organs are only active for part of the year, when conditions are best for breeding. Some animals, including humans, produce eggs and sperm at any time of the year.

For a species to continue, some of the individuals of that species must breed and replace themselves. This is the process of reproduction.

MULTIPLY AND SUBTRACT

When they reproduce, animals make a number of new individuals, usually more than two. But in many natural situations, where numbers of animals remain steady, two parents in one generation are replaced by two young in the next. This means most of the offspring produced have died. A female mouse can give birth to 50 or more babies in her lifetime. Yet only

two, on average, will become adult and themselves reproduce. In some animals the wastage rate is much higher. Some fish lay millions of eggs at a time. A plaice may lay 20 million during its life. An oyster makes 40 million eggs. Nearly all die before they reach maturity.

Others take the opposite tack, and invest heavily in the care and protection of a few young. An elephant may produce only four or five calves in her lifetime, a rhinoceros perhaps only six. An albatross may only rear four chicks. But the period of care of these young is relatively long, and they set

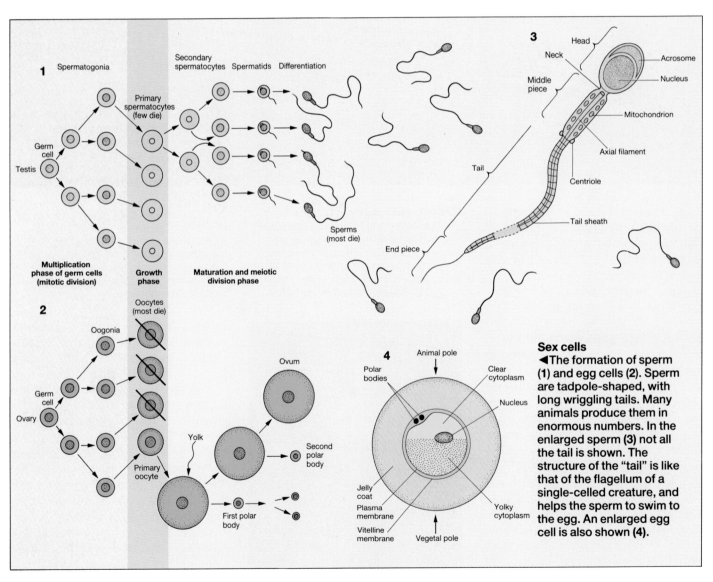

Sex cells
◄The formation of sperm (1) and egg cells (2). Sperm are tadpole-shaped, with long wriggling tails. Many animals produce them in enormous numbers. In the enlarged sperm (3) not all the tail is shown. The structure of the "tail" is like that of the flagellum of a single-celled creature, and helps the sperm to swim to the egg. An enlarged egg cell is also shown (4).

out into the world with a much higher chance of survival than the millions of scattered eggs of a fish.

BUDDING AND SPLITTING

Some animals produce new individuals that are genetically identical to themselves, simply by splitting. Many simple single-celled animals do this. Other simple animals, such as the freshwater *Hydra*, reproduce by budding. Part of the body develops an outgrowth that is eventually nipped off as a new individual. Some corals do much the same, as do sea-squirts. The cell divisions that make these new individuals are mitotic divisions (see page 76). The new individuals have exactly the same genes as the "parent."

If the parent is well adapted to the place it is living, then young produced in this way presumably will be too. Indeed this type of reproduction seems to be commonest in animals that travel hardly any distance in their lives. Those animals that disperse or travel around more commonly use sexual reproduction.

SEX AND VARIETY

In sexual reproduction, meiotic cell divisions (see page 77) produce eggs

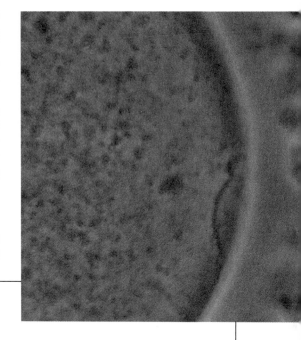

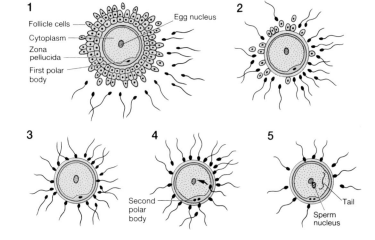

Fertilization
◄The coming together of egg and sperm. Sperm reaches the follicle cells surrounding the egg (1). The follicle cells disperse (2), and a sperm penetrates the outer layer or zona pellucida (3). A single sperm enters the egg cytoplasm (4), and the sperm nucleus and egg nucleus fuse (5).

▲An egg with a sperm inside (right).

▼Rabbit sperm seen through a microscope.

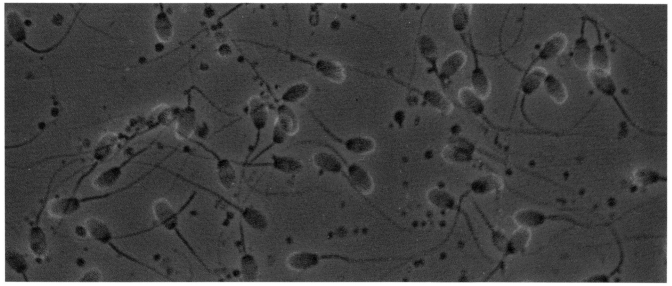

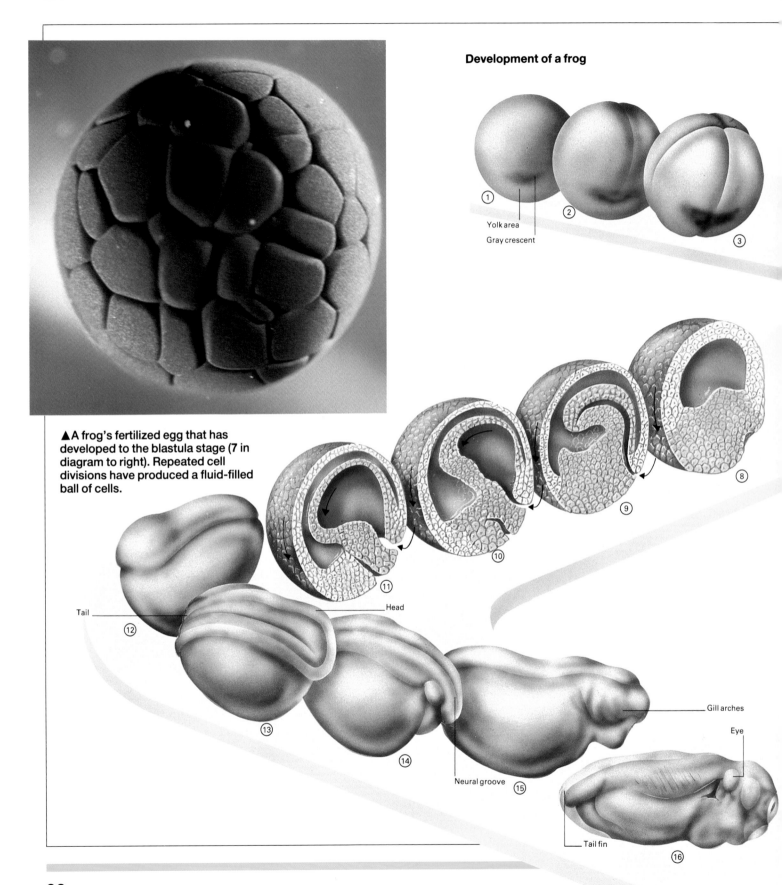

Development of a frog

Yolk area

Gray crescent

▲A frog's fertilized egg that has developed to the blastula stage (7 in diagram to right). Repeated cell divisions have produced a fluid-filled ball of cells.

Head

Tail

Neural groove

Gill arches

Eye

Tail fin

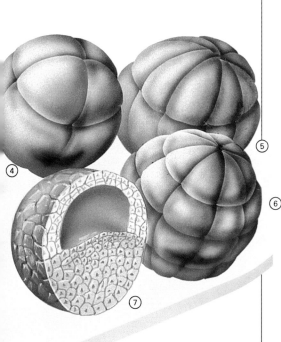

◄The egg (1) is pigmented above, the lower half yolky. At first, cell divisions are quite regular, producing 2, 4, 8, 16 and 32 cells (2–6). Then they become more irregular. Cells divide faster in the lower half, and a cavity appears in the upper half (7). A hole develops in the yolky area (8). Colored cells divide and move in through the hole to make a new inner layer (9–10). The yolk is used up until there is just a plug left (11). A groove forms on the upper surface and a head end becomes visible (12–13). The groove closes up to make a tube, and gill arches form (14–15). Then eyes and tail fin become visible (16). By hatching (17), the tadpole's gills, eyes and mouth are formed.

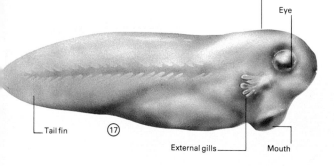

Eye

Tail fin ⑰

External gills Mouth

and sperm. Its advantage is that offspring are not genetically identical to their parents. From the variety produced, some will be less successful and disappear. But others may be very well adapted to the new place where they find themselves. These will thrive and themselves produce young.

A few animals can reproduce using either the sexual method or the simple copying of the parent, called asexual reproduction. The Water "flea" *Daphnia* is a small freshwater crustacean. In the summer, a pond will be full of female Water fleas. They may all be descended from a single female hatched in the spring. She feeds on the algae in the pond and, without needing to mate with a male, produces eggs that develop and hatch as small copies of herself.

This can carry on through several generations when life is easy in the pond, building up a huge number of individuals. But in a midsummer drought or the cold of fall, some of the females begin to produce male offspring. Mating between males and females takes place, resulting in special tough eggs that can survive the winter. From the variety of eggs produced, one will probably produce a female suited to the conditions of next year's pond.

MAKING EGGS

Eggs are the sex cells of female animals. They are usually made in special organs called ovaries. In insects and some kinds of worm, the ovaries are long tubes. Egg-producing cells are at one end, and as the egg travels along the tube, it matures. In mammals the ovaries are solid bodies

that release eggs. These travel along tubes called oviducts, and are then ready for fertilization.

Most animal eggs spend a long time in the first stage of meiotic cell division. During this, much information from the DNA is transferred to messenger RNA. This mRNA is "packaged up" and is not used until development into a new animal has begun. During the process of egg formation, yolk, special membranes and perhaps a shell may be added.

Mature eggs may be thousands of times bigger than the original egg cell, as in birds and sharks. Mammal eggs have no yolk and are comparatively small, about the size of this period.

The process of egg formation can take only a few months, as in some worms and sea urchins. It may take two years, as in a frog. Or it may take much longer. In humans, a female begins the process while just a three-month old foetus in the womb. It is finished when she is a grown woman.

MAKING SPERM

Sperm (plural also sperms or spermatozoa) are the sex cells of male animals. They are produced in organs called testes. Some snails, worms and other species are hermaphrodite, with both sets of sex organs in the same individual. Even these generally mate with another individual so the young are not identical to the parent.

In many animals, sperm are produced in even greater numbers than eggs, and huge numbers never get to fertilize an egg. A human male may produce one million million sperm in his lifetime, but probably less than ten will be able to fertilize eggs and result in children. Unlike eggs, sperm are mobile, swimming with their tails. But they carry no food supply for the young. They just contribute their genes to a new individual, when fertilization takes place.

◄King penguin and fluffy chick. Only one chick is raised by the parents during each breeding season. At the end of the season, the chick is very fat and weighs more than the parent. Once on its own, it soon uses up the fat store.

▲Young Deer mice in their grassy nest. When they were born, after a pregnancy of just three weeks, they were blind and naked. Three weeks later in their protected nest, they are furry and active, alert and aware.

STARTING OUT IN LIFE
After fertilization, when sperm and egg join together, the egg begins to make mitotic cell divisions. It divides repeatedly to form a ball of cells. The sperm's genes seem to have little effect at this stage. The egg appears to be carried through these first stages of development using messenger RNA laid down in the egg during its early development, as explained above.

Once the embryo has developed to a ball of cells there is often a series of cell movements, as layers or sheets of cells fold and twist themselves. The position of the cells in the embryo now seems to cause their development in different ways. All the cells in the developing body have the same DNA in their nuclei, but now the position in the body helps to switch on particular sets of genes.

Gradually this switching-on of genes leads to groups of cells with specialized shapes or functions. The formation of tissues and organs has begun. The animal slowly takes shape.

GROWING
Some animals hatch or are born as small replicas of their parents. Newly hatched lizards and snakes may look little different from their parents. They are smaller, of course, and not yet ready to breed, but otherwise they are easily recognized for what they are.

Many crustaceans, and some insects such as grasshoppers and cockroaches, climb a "ladder" of juvenile forms. They go through a series of shape changes, with ever-increasing size, until they become full adults.

Other animals, including starfish, crabs and many insects such as flies and butterflies, hatch looking very different to their parents. They go through one or more larval stages before turning into the adult form.

Some animals, such as most mammals and birds, and also insects, reach a more-or-less fixed adult size, after which further growth does not occur. Other animals, like reptiles and some worms, carry on growing throughout their lives.

The "investment" in reproduction is probably greatest in birds and mammals. In both of these groups, adults spend a considerable part of their lives caring for the next generation.

GLOSSARY

Adaptation Features of an animal's body or life-style that suit it to its environment.

Adult A fully developed animal that is mature and capable of breeding.

Aestivation (also **estivation**) A state of **dormancy** during the summer. Mainly undertaken by some species living in inhospitably hot, dry regions.

Amphibians Animals such as frogs and toads, which have a larval stage dependent on water and an adult stage that lives on land.

Anaerobe Describes an organism which is capable of living in the absence of oxygen. Many micro-organisms are anaerobes. Most animals are aerobes – they need oxygen.

Antibody A special type of protein formed by an animal's immune system to react with and inactivate a specific antigen (a "foreign" substance or organism). Antibodies provide protection against infections.

Aquatic Living for much, if not all, of the time in the water.

Arboreal Living for much, if not all, of the time in the trees.

Artery A blood vessel with thick, elastic walls that carries blood from the heart to the tissues and organs.

Axon The elongated part of the cell body of a nerve cell along which nerve impulses are transmitted.

Blood corpuscle A blood cell. There are two types, red (erythrocytes) and white (leucocytes).

Brain A collection of nerve cells usually at the front of the animal. It receives messages from sense organs such as eyes, interprets them, then sends messages to organs such as muscles to make the body respond in the appropriate way.

Browser An animal that feeds on the shoots, leaves and bark of shrubs and trees.

Camouflage Color and patterns on an animal's coat that allow it to blend in with its surroundings.

Carnivore A meat-eater.

Carrion Meat from a dead animal.

Cell The basic unit of an organism. Animals such as Amoeba consist of a single cell, while all others are multi-cellular.

Commensalism An association between two species such that one of them benefits without appreciable cost to the other.

Competition The contest between two or more species over such things as space and food.

Crustaceans Creatures with jointed limbs and a hard outer skin, like shrimp and krill.

Detritivore An animal that feeds on detritus, that is, on plant and animal remains.

Diurnal Active during the day.

Ecology The study of plants and animals in relation to their environment.

Egg The female reproductive cell, also known as ovum. An egg usually needs to be fertilized by a sperm before development of the embryo can begin. This may take place within or outside the female's body.

Embryo The developing egg, until it hatches. In placental mammals, such as humans, the egg hatches early inside the mother's womb and is called an embryo until it looks baby-like.

Endangered species One that is in danger of becoming extinct.

Environment The surroundings of an organism, including both the living and non-living world.

Enzyme A protein molecule that speeds up a chemical reaction without being changed itself.

Excretion The elimination of unwanted or harmful substances from the body of an organism. Getting rid of urine is excretion, but elimination of undigested food material is not.

Extinction The complete loss of a species, locally or worldwide, by natural or man-made causes.

Fauna Animal life.

Fertilization The fusion of a sperm and an egg to start development in organisms which reproduce sexually.

Filter-feeding A method of obtaining food by straining small particles from the water.

Genes The basic units of information, in chemical code, by which physical characteristics are passed from one generation to the next. Combinations of genes control an animal's size, the colour of its hair or feathers, its speed, and so on.

Genus The division of animal classification below Family and above Species.

Grazer An animal that feeds on grass.

Habitat The kind of surroundings in which an animal or plant lives.

Herbivore A plant-eater.

Hibernation Winter sleep to avoid the cold.

Hormone A chemical compound made and secreted by endocrine glands or tissues and which has a specific effect on a target organ to which it is carried by the blood.

Incubation Period during which an animal keeps an egg warm, allowing the embryo inside to grow.

Insectivore An insect-eater.

Invertebrates Animals without a backbone.

Larva Plural larvae; an early stage in the life-cycle of an animal, for example of an insect or amphibian.

Locomotion Movement from one place to another, such as swimming, flying, walking.

Mammal A class of animals whose females have mammary glands, which produce milk on which they feed their young.

Mammary gland A milk-producing organ present in mammals from which the newborn baby receives its nourishment.

Marine Living in or on the sea.

Marsupial A class of primitive mammals, whose females give birth to very underdeveloped young and raise them (usually) in a pouch.

Metabolism The processes by which chemical compounds are built up and broken down in cells with the use of energy.

Metamorphosis The change in the structure of an animal as it goes through its life-cycle, for example from egg to pupa to adult in insects.

Migration The movement of animals, especially movement over a long distance, for the purpose of feeding or breeding.

Molluscs Animals that usually have a shell, such as snails.

Niche The particular way of life of a species in a certain habitat, for example a leaf-eater in a rain forest.

Nocturnal Active during the night.

Nucleus The largest component, or organelle, of a cell. It contains all of a cell's genetic material and so controls the cell's activity.

Omnivore An animal with a varied diet, which eats both plants and animals.

Parasitism One species living on or inside another one, feeding at the host's expense.

Pheromone An air-borne chemical smell produced by an animal that can be detected in minute quantities by another. It acts as a signal and produces a reaction in the receiving animal. Commonly used as an attractant between the sexes.

Plankton Microscopic plants (phytoplankton) and animals (zooplankton) that live in water and drift with the current.

Predator An animal that hunts other animals for food.

Prey An animal that is hunted.

Primates An order of animals that includes monkeys, apes and humans.

Rain forest Tropical and sub-tropical forest that has plentiful rainfall all year round.

Reflex An automatic response made by an animal to something in its surroundings, such as the pupil of the eye contracting in bright light.

Reptiles Cold-blooded animals with a scaly skin, such as snakes, lizards crocodiles and tortoises.

Respiration Internal respiration represents the processes involved in the production of energy within cells of the body. External respiration is the uptake of oxygen and the release of carbon dioxide by an animal.

Rodent A mammal belonging to the animal order that includes rats, mice and squirrels.

Scavenger An animal that feeds on the remains of carcasses that others have abandoned.

Species The division of animal classification below Genus. A group of animals with broadly similar body structure and characteristics and that can breed together.

Symbiosis An association between two species in which both gain some form of benefit.

Terrestrial Spending most of the time on the ground.

Vein A thin-walled blood vessel in which blood flows from the tissues and organs to the heart.

Vertebrates Animals with a backbone.

INDEX

FURTHER READING

Alexander, R. McN. (1979), *The Invertebrates*, Cambridge University Press, Cambridge.

Alexander, R. McN. (1981), *The Chordates* (2nd edn), Cambridge University Press, Cambridge.

Alexander, R. McN. (1986), *The Encyclopedia of Animal Biology*, Facts on File, New York.

Arms, K. and Camp P. S. (1982), *Biology*, Saunders College Publishing, Philadelphia.

Barrington, E. J. W. (1979), *Invertebrate Structure and Function* (2nd edn), Nelson, London.

Barth, R. H. and Broshears, R. E. (1982), *The Invertebrate World*, Saunders College Publishing, Philadelphia.

Buckle, J. W. (1983), *Animal Hormones*, Arnold, London.

Calow, P. (1978), *Life Cycles*, Chapman & Hall, London.

Cohen, J. and Massey, B. (1982), *Living Embryos* (3rd edn), Pergamon, Oxford.

deDuve, C, (1984), *A Guided Tour of the Living Cell*, Scientific American Books, New York.

Gordon, M. S. Bartholomew, G. A., Grinnell, A. D. Jorgensen,

C. B. and White, F.N. (1982), *Animal Physiology. Principles and Adaptations* (4th edn), Macmillan, New York.

Gray, J. (1968), *Animal Locomotion*, Weidenfeld & Nicolson, London.

Gregory, R. L. (1978), *Eye and Brain* (3rd edn), McGraw-Hill, New York.

Hardy, R. N. (1983), *Homeostasis* (2nd edn), Arnold, London.

Hildebrand, M, Bramble, D. M. Liem, K. F. and Wake, D. B, (eds) (1985), *Functional Vertebrate Morphology*, Harvard University Press, Cambridge, Massachusetts.

Jennings, J. B. (1972), *Feeding, Digestion and Assimilation in Animals* (2nd edn), Macmillan, London.

Kimball, J. W. (1984), *Cell Biology* (3rd edn), Addison-Wesley, Reading, Massachusetts.

McMahon, T. A. (1984), *Muscles, Reflexes and Locomotion*, Princeton University Press, Princeton, New Jersey.

Ruppell, G. (1977), *Bird Flight*, Van Nostrand Reinhold, New York.

Schmidt-Nielsen, K. (1972), *How Animals Work*, Cambridge University Press, Cambridge.

Schmidt-Nielsen, K. (1983), *Animal Physiology: Adaptation and Environment* (3rd edn), Cambridge University Press, Cambridge.

Scientific American (1979), *Hormones and Reproductive Behavior*, Freeman, San Francisco.

Stanier, M. W., Mount, L. E., and Bligh, J. (1984), *Energy Balance and Temperature Regulation*, Cambridge University Press, Cambridge.

Villee, C. A., Solomon, E. P, and Davis, P. W., (1985), *Biology*, Saunders College Publishing, Philadelphia.

Weibel, E. R. (1984), *The Pathway for Oxygen, Structure and Function in the Mammalian Respiratory System*, Harvard University Press, Cambridge, Massachusetts.

Young, J. Z. (1978), *Programs of the Brain*, Oxford University Press, Oxford.

Young, J. Z. (1981), *The Life of Vertebrates* (3rd edn) Clarendon, Oxford.

Wickler, W. (1968) Mimicry in Plants and Animals, Weldenfeld & Nicolson. London.

Wilson, E. O. (1971) *The Insect Societies*, Belknap Press, Harvard.